A walking journey across North America

keremeye'us

Joseph Woodcock

Brenda

Thanks and I hope
you enjoy!

ISBN

978-1-4602-3827-1 (Hardcover)

978-1-4602-3828-8 (Paperback)

978-1-4602-3829-5 (eBook)

Produced by:

FriesenPress

Suite 300 – 852 Fort Street

Victoria, BC, Canada V8W 1H8

www.friesenpress.com

Distributed to the trade by The Ingram Book Company

For Jessica and Michael

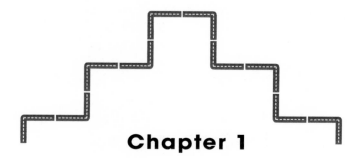

Chapter 1

I am not sure when this story began, as the edges are tattered shreds of fabric running outward against the colour and texture of my early life. Looking back, though, I can't help but feel it is all connected, as if all roads led to that place and that time when I set out on a great walking trek across the continent of North America. Like the beginning, the end, I think, may extend far beyond what is written here. I believe these words reflect a juncture, a crossing point, where paths intersect. This story is about that brief time, when all roads came back together and I was able to turn and look back on each one. This is a story of a walking journey, but even more so, it is a story about a gift I received and, without knowing it, how I shared this gift.

One evening my dad, Stew, and his spouse Nancy had drawn the curtains, settled into their chairs, and struggled through the simple operation of the VCR. Once successful, both sat in guilty silence and watched the host play with dolls and props on a seniors' sex show. As callers phoned in to the show with questions regarding everything and anything to do with sex, Nancy and Stew were riveted to the television. Not able to fully navigate the remote, they watched the commercials in eager anticipation of the show's resumption. It was during the second commercial break that Nancy turned to Stew. About to ask him a question, she froze for a few seconds and then said to him, "Your face is falling off."

My sister phoned me the next day and told me the news that Dad had suffered a very serious stroke and was struggling for his life. I arrived on Vancouver Island a couple of days later after driving from northern British Columbia. Stew's condition was extremely poor but at the same time he was stable. The first two weeks we waited for improvement and, along the way, learned about the effects of a stroke and began to digest the decisions that lay ahead of us. I had temporarily moved in with Nancy at their two-bedroom retirement unit and as the weeks melded together it was clear that their lives had changed forever.

Not able to predict what was ahead of us, I quit my job and made personal preparations for the possibilities. My father spent two months in hospital and when he was released he required constant care. A few months later, Dad and I had moved into a small one-bedroom apartment in a seniors' building and Nancy occupied a small, bright room across the road in a new assisted-living complex. There were ups and downs, but generally my father's mobility and overall health slowly improved and so began the routine and the day-to-day tasks associated with caring for the elderly.

Time seemed to stand still and I focused on the future. I knew that this event was a milestone—that it marked a pivot point. I was always able to shed the negatives of the past and look forward. In taking stock, I bundled together a series of adverse personal events and in one deposit cast them aside. So in the silence of the early evenings, with the West Coast rains falling through the darkness, I began to conceive a path forward.

I had always been a passionate reader and admirer of explorers, especially those with little means. As a child, hiking in the low mountains of the Cowichan Valley, I imagined setting out on a walking adventure someday. So, with nothing but time

Joseph Woodcock

on my hands, I began the process of fulfilling that boyhood dream and began planning and preparing for the venture. I did not know when my father would be well enough or if he ever would, but if the opportunity came, I simply wanted to walk from there and head east.

Right from the start I knew that it was not a test or a task. I genuinely did not have a route or time of year planned. I never did the math on distance or space and never calculated the monetary costs or even placed worth on completion. For me, it seemed that just to walk was enough. Realistically though, I knew that I could not spend months and cover thousands of kilometers with little more than a bed roll and a flask of tea. What energy I conserved with regard to personal mental and physical preparation, I spent on what tools would be required. Simply put, I did not want to try to predict what was going to happen, but instead spent my time developing the equipment that would allow me to react to challenges as they arose.

I understood early on that my trek would require a fair bit of equipment, so I concentrated firstly on how I was going to carry it. I searched the Internet and read up on others who had made such a journey, but I never wavered far from a cart of some sort. I had spent several months in rural China and had seen how vast quantities of goods were still transported short distances via a rickshaw or variation. I realised that an adaptation to the rickshaw would be the most advantageous; I began to build from that idea.

It came about quickly, as I soon found a strong bike trailer and converted it to a base frame. I then bought one-inch-square aluminum tubing and, on the deck of our apartment, cut the angles needed to make the pulling frame. I had a local person weld up the joints and soon I was pulling around a two-wheeled cart. From there the rickshaw grew to meet my equipment requirements. Two additional components were also needed: a harness system so I could pull from my chest, and a hood or bonnet under which I could shield myself from the elements.

The construction took several months of tinkering and

keremeye'us

modifications, but in the end the rickshaw was impressive and functional. It could easily carry in excess of two hundred pounds, could come apart and be shipped within its self and provided shelter from the weather. Of course, there were missteps and changes along the way, but the rickshaw would prove to provide what I needed in the long term. In the short term the planning and construction of the rickshaw offered me therapy and kept me busy as my father continued his recovery.

In early October, sixteen months after his stroke, my father asked me if he could move next door to be with Nancy. His health and mobility, though vastly improved, was still tenuous and we talked about it off and on for a few days. In the end though, he made the decision to join Nancy and almost overnight the assisted living staff confirmed a space for him. It was a positive thing, but inside I knew he would deteriorate without the one-on-one care. We had visited Nancy every day and in that year we had seen people come in and, of course, leave forever. So on the tenth of October, we moved his few things across the street and I gave our apartment a decent clean. The final night was spent sleeping on the hardwood floor in my sleeping bag. In front of the sliding door, the rickshaw cast a long shadow back toward me and I wondered where we would take each other.

In the predawn chill of that October morning I stepped out of the lobby of the seniors' apartment complex. To the muted cheer of a few supporters who braved the early morning darkness, I strapped on the yoke and slid under the bonnet and, thanking everyone, I waved toward the assisted living complex across the street where Stew and Nancy were sleeping. The pelting rain of the previous days had stopped and now the stars and partial moon moved beside me as I crept through the streets. Soon I was out of the city itself and, in my first minor test, climbed the small rise of Lakes Road Hill. Once at the top, I stopped and took a final glance at the lights below with a sense of satisfaction.

Stew was a man of exceedingly few words and after his

stroke he said remarkably little. In the year since I started to build the rickshaw I had talked to him every day about its progress and what my plan was. Day after day he would sit in his chair and watch me adjust and construct. As this was going on, I would talk to him slowly and loudly about what I was doing. He never spoke a word about it and never asked a question until the rig was entirely finished and fully loaded. On that day, I had packed the rickshaw up with everything and strapped myself in. I walked back and forth in from of him and waited for a comment. Then, after a long period of silence and with a cantankerous scowl, he barked out, "You won't even make it up Lakes Road Hill." Laughing, I turned toward the east and muttered, "How's that you cranky old fart?"

I boarded the small ferry at Crofton, walked across Salt Spring Island, and then continued on to another ferry bound for Tsawwassen. The lack of sleep and the undulating rise and fall of the roads of the island took its toll and by the time I reached the Tsawwassen terminal on the mainland it was evening and I was looking for a place to set up my tent. Of course, there was no spot, so I chose a small isolated patch of grass under a large sign that read "No Camping." In the morning I encountered an old English woman who was walking her three exceptionally large dogs. The dogs were friendly but the old woman was not. I tried to strike up a pleasant conversation as her dogs strained at their leashes trying to get into the tent. I thought they were just curious, but the old snag informed me that her dogs took a crap each morning on that very patch of grass and "No bloody vagrant is going to take that away from them."

The next few days I worked my way through the lower Fraser Valley trying to stay off the main roads. Eventually I found a bath and soft bed at the home of one of my nieces. The sunny weather would be ending soon so, after staying a night in a Walmart parking lot, I left the suburbs behind me and paralleled the busy TransCanada Highway along a series of service roads. It was on one of these service roads that I hit my first obstacle and experienced the first of many lessons. The map

keremeye'us

I was using clearly showed that the road I was on crossed the river, but in reality it did not. The bridge was gone and the road continued on the other side. So I had a decision to make: go back the way I came and cross another bridge miles away, or walk a short distance over grass to the TransCanada Highway. Once on the main highway, I could cross over its bridge, then hop back over to the side road and continue on.

I hardly needed to think about it—without too much hesitation I stumbled through the grass and stood soon beside a steady stream of two-lane traffic running at 120 kilometers per hour. I took stock of the situation and tried to calculate the time it would take me to run from one end of the bridge to the other, as there were no sidewalks. I then pretended I had run a few times and judged how much space is required before the next vehicle caught up. It was tight. So there I stood for a few minutes looking at the far end of the bridge, which was where I wanted to be and which seemed like such a short distance.

When I saw an opening I bolted and almost immediately wished I had not. I had presumed that the vehicles in the left lane would stay in that lane but they also saw an opening and at least two tried to swing into the right-hand lane. There was a barrage of screaming and yelling, squealing tires, and evasive action, but I could not look back, let alone stop. As the end of the abutment neared I focused on the sanctuary of the gravel shoulder ahead. A few more long strides and I was there, but not by much, as the space I had just vacated disappeared under the wheels of a large and angry transport truck.

Sitting on the shoulder I panted and heaved and swore that I would never take a chance like that again and thanked God for sparing me. As I got to my feet, it became apparent to me that I had risked my life in vain. On the other side of the bridge I crossed from the access road to the main highway easily, but here there was a deep ravine between where I was and where I wanted to be. I looked farther down the main highway and right away it crossed another bridge, but longer. I was not going to do that again, especially since I had just thanked heaven for the last safe crossing. So it became apparent that I would have to carry everything down this great bloody hill and then pack it all the way up the other side. Luckily, I thought, it was just knee-high grass—it could have been brambles or something even more unappealing. In fact, it was just grass and a steep hill. I had equipped my rickshaw with brakes so there would be no need to unpack.

I started down and found the going quite good. The brakes locked up the tires and I could work them back and forth to both slow and steer my descent. A minute later I was at the bottom and quite tickled with how well things had gone to that point. Now brimming with pride and self-confidence, I started the slow climb up the other side and almost immediately was stunned with how steep it was and how far I had to go. Everything I had in my favour on the descent was now a negative—the grass tangled in the spokes and the loose gravel made my footing difficult. But soon I had climbed partway up, and then, ten minutes later, I was halfway up. I gingerly pressed forward and with each step the rickshaw creaked and moaned under the two hundred pounds of supplies. Fifteen minutes later I neared the top of the hill. My lungs howled and my legs and entire frame cried out for relief. I knew that I could make it in one last burst and drove my shoes into the earth and leaned into the harness.

On the climb, my body was almost parallel to the rise and I hung onto any grass or shrubs I could grasp. I never thought about angles or physics of the climb, only that I was scrambling upward. I should have been thinking about the angles and the physics, because when I reached the crest of the hill and stood up the angles and physics changed. I was on level ground, but the rickshaw and its cargo were at a forty-five degree angle and that, along with my now vertical stance, tipped the fulcrum.

At first, and only for an instant, the sensation of being aloft was magical, almost mystic. The mystic part evaporated when I realised I was strapped into a teeter-totter and going over the crest of the ravine backwards. The crest of the hill, which I had

keremeye'us

worked so hard to reach, slipped away from my view and the pain of the climb was replaced with sheer panic and nausea. I felt the tail of the rickshaw strike the ground but by then, the entire unit was over centre and my weight acted as the energy. Grasping as best as I could, I braced for a backwards upside-down impact. When I did strike the earth, the canopy caved in and drove the canvas and aluminum supports around my head blinding me from any sense of space.

The initial impact hit with such force that the fully loaded rickshaw trailer had swung up above me with enough momentum to crest and then begin to fall down the side of the hill. The situation was like that of a Slinky going over an edge. I think I was screaming. When the trailer hit the ground the second time, I was flung upward with tremendous force—and I knew the ride was just beginning. Thus started a series of catapulting plunges down the ravine; I managed to stay somewhat cognisant of the first three of four full rotations.

I did not know at first, but I had come to rest at the bottom of the ravine with the trailer tail on the ground. I was still strapped in and hanging backwards and upside down, with the canopy wrapped around my head. The only thing of me that was exposed were my legs which resembled two wilting flower stems sticking out of a crinkled gift bag; one to the left and the other to the right. I am not sure of the length of time that I hung there in silence, but in formulating the events that took place during that period, I guess that it must have been about fifteen minutes.

The distance between the first bridge that I ran across and the second bridge that I did not was very short. The traffic, which was speeding along, would exit the first bridge and then almost immediately feel the deck of second. The ravine to the right fell away steeply and there were some bushes and obstacles limiting a clear view of where I was. So for a person in a speeding car, the view of my tangled rickshaw would be nothing more than a blink. Because of the bridges and lack of shoulder space there is no opportunity to stop. There was also a recognition factor. I mean, one generally does not see too many rickshaws in western Canada, so the calls to 911 were fractured and vague.

In a small, rural restaurant, a young police officer had just sat down at the counter. The daily special was a mushroom burger and the officer had anticipated biting into one all morning. Pouring a bit of cream into his coffee and relishing the quiet time between traffic duties, he started to read a magazine. It was then that his radio began to squawk regarding an incident on the highway. The operator informed him that there had been some sort of accident and, though each caller had explained the scene differently, each could see legs protruding from the wreckage. The young officer dashed from the restaurant to the patrol car and, with lights flashing and siren blaring, set off at high speed toward the carnage.

On the way he received constant updates from the 911 operator regarding others who, for a split second, witnessed the wreck. At first, it was thought that it was some sort of tractor rollover as the canopy colour was close to that of John Deere green. When the officer heard this he banged on the dash, scolding those God damn Dutch farmers for letting their kids drive the equipment. Then the next report was that a hang-glider or ultralight had crashed, as they are a common sight in the blue skies of that area. Then came stories of a tent trailer, a raft, another tractor, something from a circus, a canoe, another tractor, and, finally, the sidecar of a motorbike—the witness had no idea where the actual motorbike had gone. The young officer tried to assimilate all this as he dodged in and out of traffic on his way to the scene.

At some point, I had gathered my thoughts and managed to free myself from the wreck. Though I was bruised and battered with a few small cuts and abrasions, nothing seemed to be broken. My first reaction as I hit the ground was to get some distance between myself and the rickshaw, as if it may burst into flames. I found a small bush nearby and stretched out in the shade. It was peaceful there in the ravine—almost serene in comparison to the flurry of activity that was taking place among the first responders.

As each varying report was entered into the 911 computer, it prompted alerts to other departments who, in turn, started their early response procedures, which included: the Workers' Compensation Board (in regard to farm workers), provincial ambulance and paramedics, firefighters and rescuers—the word "canoe" initiated River Rescue, the word "ravine" prompted the Mountain Rescue Centre; the National Transportation Centre becomes involved regarding anything that flies; and, finally, a series of blind searches for the phrase "something from a circus."

Luckily, the young officer opted to take the back roads and arrived on the site earlier than expected via the service road I was trying to reach. His first concern was for any injuries or fatalities. Once that information was confirmed and relayed back to the 911 centre, he quickly tried to assess the situation for a further transmission. He came down into the ravine and I explained what had happened. I think I had to go through it several times. At the top of the hill, the open patrol car door allowed the radio transmissions to echo to us below and one by one the operator issued "stand down, stand down" directives to scrambling departments and agencies. Finally, after a few minutes of coded radio transmissions, the officer's cell phone rang.

He looked first at the call display, winced, and then answered. "Yes, sir...no, sir....no, sir," he replied. "Rickshaw, sir...yes, rickshaw...no motor, sir...." Turning to me he asked my speed and I replied, "About four kilometers per hour." "Yes sir...four kilometres per hour...confirmed...yes a rollover at four kilometers per hour. No sir, no sign of drugs or alcohol." Looking quite pained, he continued. "No, sir...no sidecar... nothing motorized...no, sir....nothing to do with a circus...yes, sir, a Canadian citizen." And so it went until the young officer helped me gather up what had fallen off of the trailer and then, together, we managed to pull the rickshaw to the road above.

Once on the roadway I apologised continuously to the officer as I straightened the canopy supports and strapped on the loose equipment. We chatted for some time before he drove off, no doubt thinking again of his mushroom burger and some peace and quiet before tackling the paperwork required to put the incident to bed. I took stock of what had happened and could feel the next day's pain, so I pulled out the map and looked for a spot on which to set up camp a bit early. That evening I stripped down and washed and bandaged my wounds. Lying down upon my cot I took shallow, painful breaths, which were to haunt me in the days ahead as I entered my first real test in climbing from Hope to Alison Summit. But it was also a good feeling—one of adventure and adversity and above all, something unexpected and completely different. I felt truly alive.

The next day, I got on the road a bit later than normal as I relaxed and washed up my laundry in a local stream. I could feel the weather changing so I wanted to take the few hours of sunshine to dry my clothes. Once washed, I hung them all over the rickshaw and then started off in at a slow and tender pace through the back roads. As I passed through one town I must have been quite a sight. The canopy and some of the frame was still bent and it was covered with laundry. I was very sore and hobbled and scuffled at every step. At some point I must have passed some men working in a yard but did not notice them. Apparently they took note of my wretched and tattered appearance and between them they came to several conclusions.

As I neared the edge of town the road narrowed to allow a level railway crossing. As I crossed the tracks a large flat deck truck roared past me and came to an abrupt stop on the other side. The door swung open and a large, very fit man jumped out and came walking toward me quickly. I did not have time to react as he threw his arms in the air in disgust and distain and then in a deep Dutch accent yelled, "What happened, what happened to you?" I was taken aback and, of course, being Dutch he did not wait for an answer but continued on with the rant on my general appearance and the situation I was in. I literally

keremeye'us

could not get a word in to my defence. His voice even grew louder and he was clearly agitated. I gave up trying to reply but was wondering where this was coming from as he seemed both aggressive and at the same time, very sympathetic with my situation, whatever he thought that was. Then it all came out when he threw his hands to the sky and howled, "You bitches, see what you do?"

Apparently, a woman had, at some point, done him wrong and this had brought on some depression, which in turn led to anger and then a spell in the local jail. It all went south on him afterward and, up to that point, every negative event was the fault of a woman. When he saw me shuffling down the road with what looked like everything I owned, there was only one conclusion—a woman had driven me to this. "I mean look at you, you are pathetic." He went on to tell me that I was perhaps of some worth before all this happened but now I was relegated to wander as a bum. Eventually, he calmed down some but forcibly made me take twenty dollars for a warm meal and coffee. "No booze, you have got to promise me that." Looking me square in the eye, I agreed and shuffled off as he continued to mutter and fume on the tracks until I was out of sight. I took his advice and a few kilometers later had a pleasant lunch at a local diner with the twenty dollars.

A few days later I was in the town of Hope and stayed the night in a small motel. I was starting to feel a little better and after a couple of hot baths and a good sleep I stepped out into the pouring rain for the start of my ascent to Alison Pass in Manning Park. I did not leave too early as my goal for that day was only the base of the Hope Slide. This was a good decision as the initial climb was difficult and my ribs ached with every breath.

As I pulled the cart upward into the clouds I was accompanied by a steady stream of gravel trucks moving contaminated earth from the old Expo site in Vancouver to a site near Princeton. The drivers were South Asian and completely bewildered by me struggling up the steep grades in the sleet, pulling

Joseph Woodcock

a rickshaw. Their speed on the ascent was very slow, so we waved back and forth and they chatted to each other using CB Radios. That night, as I set up my tent, some stopped on their return trip and we had a great conversation. The next day and every day until Princeton, at least one would stop and give me food that his wife had bundled up for me. It was wonderful and generous, and much appreciated.

For the next two days the weather was cold and clear. I climbed upward through the steep switchbacks, crossing the swollen Skagit River several times and was enthralled and excited by the views. The second night of my ascent I camped alongside the river and drank tea under the embrace of only the stars. The dark frame of the vertical cliffs and soft silence of the mountains seemed to welcome me back home. The temperature fell just below freezing but I lay warm and safe in my tent and after several days of fatigue, I sensed a new strength within me. The morning brought excitement, as I knew the summit was within reach. But there was also delay and laughter, as the cold had frozen all my tent poles together at the joints. I tried in vain to pull them apart but finally had to unpack my gas stove and thaw each joint so that they would fold.

In the late afternoon I reached Alison Summit and camped in the Highways Maintenance yard at the invitation of the crew. In the morning I walked the few kilometers to Manning Park Lodge and enjoyed a big breakfast of bacon and eggs. As I was eating a group of people gathered around the rickshaw. Once inside the restaurant we struck up a conversation. This group had just completed the Pacific Crest Trail and had hiked from the Mexico/US border through the various mountain ranges to Manning Park—a six-month journey. It was great to hear their stories and experiences.

By late morning I was again enjoying the walk on the slow descent through what was now a much dryer environment as the dense coastal forest cover was now replaced with pine and aspen. But it was more than an environmental change—I could feel a swagger and confidence in my step, along with a real sense of peace with where I was at that time and place.

As I neared Princeton a few days later the weather was changing. It was late October and I enjoyed every step, knowing the trek for this year would soon end. I had only walked for fifteen days but it was a legitimate test for the coming year ahead. I stored much of my gear in Princeton and a few weeks later was in Northern Alberta working on a pipeline. I worked the winter and eagerly waited for the spring and for the freedom I had tasted. Sometimes on the construction project if there was a vista I would catch myself staring off into the distance. My partner would laugh and yell up at me, "Hey, Joe, are you rickshawing?"

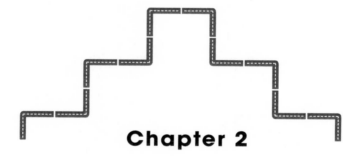

Chapter 2

On February 25, I began my second season of walking. It was too early and I knew that, but I longed to be trekking again. I had reliable equipment and clothing and had no time frames

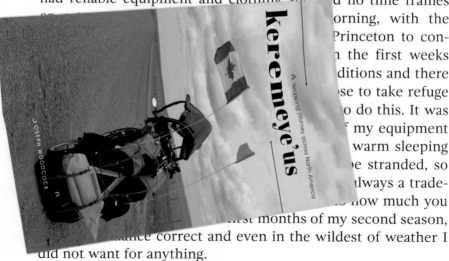

orning, with the
Princeton to con-
the first weeks
ditions and there
se to take refuge
o do this. It was
my equipment
warm sleeping
e stranded, so
lways a trade-
how much you
months of my second season,
ce correct and even in the wildest of weather I did not want for anything.

There was also a process taking place, one that had its seeds in the days after reaching Alison Summit the year before. For me that short season was a test of equipment, and it had a time frame, as I knew the winter was coming. This year, as I paced along the Similkameen River, there was none of that and my journey had no rules. I knew that I was going to travel in a general eastward direction but that was only because I started in the west with the Pacific at my back. With this lack of margins, the second season had a boundless feel. This is something so rare, a sensation that brings on minor bouts of anxiety, but is also tempered with desire. This desire, it seems, was not rooted in distance or time, but in the lack of it and it became an enigma, something of another dimension for me. Whatever this calm feeling was, it spawned other lost or not-yet-found sensations. One of them was reminiscence—my trek produced an explosion of long-forgotten memories. These memories, which occupy parts of this book, are as much a part of the journey as the walk itself. The trek became a vehicle or transport in which to look inward and the true adventures were the quiet times— solitude with a cup of tea and a piece of frozen chocolate.

One cold afternoon I tugged my rickshaw down a small path to the bank of the river. It was between storms. I made a small fire and changed my wet clothes. I roasted a hard cheese and onion sandwich over the flames. My kettle began to sing and I placed it back a bit from the glow, dropped in a tea bag, and then found my mug in eager anticipation. As I listened to the crackle of the fire, the soft surge of water under ice and a distant icy silence of windswept peaks, a tender flutter of wings along the opposite river bank drew me in. As the small group of birds moved from one stand of trees to another, their size, shape, and undulating flight was unmistakable. I smiled and then found it hard to breathe as I was caught in a vibrant memory of my childhood.

I was perhaps five years old, at home with my mother. We lived in a small house at the top of the CPR Hill in Revelstoke, British Columbia. I was the youngest of seven children and not yet in school, so I spent the days in the skunk cabbage swamp beside our home with our dog Blackie. Spring was long in those days, there in the Columbia Valley nestled tight between the Monashee and

Selkirk Mountain ranges. It was a contrast, those days in March as piles of snow still corralled the streets, but the warm spring sun upon the metal roofs below stung our eyes. Glaciers were months from being seen under the weight of heavy snows, but on our hill, with Revelstoke below, each day brought new sights and smells and in the naked canopy of cottonwood and dense carpet of devil's club, young shoots and ferns crowded along the patchwork of mud, jarring and harassing the last, ragged edges of winter.

My mother was a war bride. Born in Scotland, she met my father during the Second World War in London. She was of immense intelligence and devoured books, sometimes one a day, on every subject. She did not drive so I remember walking back and forth to the library constantly, each time chatting with neighbours and friends along the way. This bond with the library and that of my inquisitiveness formed a connection, a link from the natural world around me to the written word. More than curious, the appreciation and wonder of all natural life and how it was expressed and explained would consume me for years to come. It may have begun in the swamp behind our home, chasing beetles through the mud, but one small incident directed my young energy down a path that would shape the rest of my entire life.

One spring day there was a thump against our picture window. Our family dog Blackie bounded toward the door and of course I followed. He was well ahead of me and was nosing around the base of the stairs outside. Upon investigation I found a small bird that had flown into the window and was, I thought, dead. I brought it to my mother and she was able to revive it. There was incredible joy when I took the bird to the edge of the deck and it flew away.

When my father came home I told him the story and he asked me what kind of bird it was as the forest teemed with so many. I was at a loss and felt disappointed at my missed opportunity. My mother said that the next day, while at the library, we could have a look at the bird books and try to find out the bird's identity, and so it started.

From that day on it was a challenge to not only save the birds that hit our window, and there were many, but also to identify them.

My mother had devised a system to up our odds of success. When a bird hit the window, Blackie and I would rush out and retrieve it. In the kitchen, my mother would quickly drive the bird into a sock and then place it in the dark, cool space under the sink beside an always-fermenting batch of dandelion wine or potato champagne. I always snuck a peek at the bird before it went into the sock and in the hour or so it was recovering, I would haul out all the bird books I could get from the library and try to identify it. Of course, the library had no field guides and sometimes I was looking at photos of pink flamingos and toucans but it was a process that taught me about the world as we ruled out penguins and others due to their geographical locations.

One day there was a terrific crash against the window as I was watching The Friendly Giant on TV. Even Blackie stood erect and a bit frozen. Then we ran out of the door and down the outside steps to the commotion of a large bird trapped between the stairwell and siding of the house. Blackie was in my way and it was almost impossible to yank him back as he had no collar and had position on me. My mother, who had been drinking and was in that phase between contentment and bitter disappointment, scolded me from the top of the landing at my inaction. "Get ya mitts round it, ya daft wee bastard."

So, in one lunge over the dog, I was able to pounce on the bird and hold it under my weight. With my mother cuffing me, Blackie out of his mind, and the bird struggling to free itself, I had little time to have a look at it before my mother slapped it into a work sock and fired it under the sink. What I did see though was something new for me. I had learned to notice certain things and to categorise markings and in the seconds of hysteria as my mother unleashed a barrage of insults and swatted at me, I noted a few main characteristics, but missed the most prominent one.

For reasons of spite, my mother left the bird in the sock and in the cupboard for a long period of time. She was entering the stage of her own reminiscence, and it was dark and bitter. As she drank, she muttered, occasionally stamping her foot on the wood floor. I knew the cycle was changing, it always did, but I wanted to see the *bird fly away before I slipped into the shadows myself to wait out the insanity of the evening and night ahead. Finally, Blackie was able to induce the next move as he pawed and sniffed at the cupboard door. "Get to bugger ya filthy midden," she grumbled as she steered his nose away from the door. To his credit though, Blackie persisted and eventually he wore her down.*

When my mother brought out the sock it flexed and danced with the bird clearly ready to get back to the forest. The extraction from the sock was difficult and the bird fought every tactic to release the wool from its claws and then finally its bill. When he was free of the sock I was taken aback with the beauty and health of the creature. Its colours were vivid and fluid and even its demeanour was so different. Others were still somewhat weary and lethargic, but this species was wild and even angry.

Instantly, though, my mother let out a gasp and brought my attention to the bill. Its beak seemed heavily damaged from the impact of the window, in fact, it resembled something from the Bugs Bunny and Roadrunner Hour as the top went one way and the lower the other. There was silence as we pondered its fate. I am sure my mother would have just let the bird go into the wild if it was not for her being quite drunk. But being quite drunk, she decided to adjust the beak a bit as to give it a fighting chance. So the operation began, there on the kitchen table.

Pulling out the junk drawer, my mother fished about and finally took out a rusty old set of pliers. Quickly rolling a fag and pouring a tall mug of home brew, she held the bird on its back and tried to fit her tiny hands around the expanding grip of the tool. With a rollie hanging off her bottom lip and balancing only on her high heels, which she reserved for times of drinking, she pushed back her black hair and went in. It was horrific. I could not directly look and moved to the end of the table to try frantically to find the bird in the books we had. Even Blackie—who, along with all of us kids, watched my dad pull out his friend Hans' molar at this same table with those same pliers—looked nauseous.

As my mother struggled and fought with the bird, all the time suggesting she was helping it, I continued my search for something

keremeye'us

in the books and in the paper and magazine clippings we had collected. After about ten minutes it sounded like my mother was winning, Blackie had to lie down and following with my eyes, a clipping floated from the pile to the floor and on it, I saw the image I was after.

Dropping the rest of the books I retrieved the clipping from under my mother's heels and sat there stunned on the floor. As my mother finished up she stepped back to admire her work. The bird lay silent, its beak somewhat straighter, somewhat. Its eyes, though, resembled that of a Chameleon, bulging and moving independently of each other, taking in the surroundings in separate images. Its head seemed offset to its neck and when it opened its beak, its left foot and right wing stuck out. Still, my mother concluded it was a hell of an improvement to what we started with and commended herself with another mug of beer.

Still quite smug about the outcome, my mother noted Blackie heading for the door with his tail between his legs and then she looked at me who stood paralysed a few feet away, still holding the clipping. "Did ye find the wee bird there ya daft little prick? Come on now, let us have a look." I don't remember if I said anything but my mother tugged the clipping from my grasp and held it to the light of the kitchen window. I was not able to read the caption at the bottom of the photo, one did not need to, but my mother read it aloud. "A common migrant to the Columbia Valley, the red crossbill displays its highly specialised beak designed for foraging seeds from the cones of conifers."

Grabbing the edge of the counter, my mother looked as if she had committed a war crime and instantly grew stark and pale. The crossbill kept moving its beak and with this movement its left leg and right wing. It was not making a sound, but to me, it looked like it wanted to give up the location of some resistance fighters if only the whole thing would just end. My mother drew in on another fag and tried to compose herself but she was clearly rattled by the photo and caption. She read it several times not actually able to believe it.

Then there was a long silence and I am not sure what she was

thinking but at one point she seemed to eye me up and down suspi-
ciously. Then, with a bang of the screen door in the breeze, it was
over. In a few steps she had picked up the crossbill and, throwing
the bird off of the porch like a bocce ball, it disappeared from view
below us. There was a pregnant pause for a few seconds and then
the crossbill appeared over the top of the railing making a tight and
fast circular flight between the porch and the large cottonwood tree
across the yard.

Even though it was flying, all it could achieve was a small
radius circle at high speed. I felt it go past my face at least three
times, its one eye looking around as if it was a stowaway on the side
of a crop duster. Then with even a tighter circle it gained altitude
and continued to do so until it cleared the trees and then, nudged
by the slight breeze, slipped over the canopy and disappeared.
Another uneasy pause and then my mother concluded, "Right y'are
then, all is well. The wee bugger is well enough to fuck around."

After several days of following the Similkameen River I crossed over to the town of Osoyoos and on March 1, under crisp and clear skies, I began the winding journey up Antichrist Mountain. The weather reports called for wet snows that evening so I relished in the opportunity to at least conquer some of the climb in dry conditions. The arid desert air slipped easily through me and together with dry socks, the pains and discomforts of the first week's travel were starting to wane. I took my time and appreciated the views and the relative warmth of the sun. It was a fabulous day.

In the late afternoon, after leaving the vistas behind, I entered the pine forests and continued to gain altitude. The weather now was degrading quickly and as the sleet began to fall I found a camp location. Normally I would camp just off of the road in a flat, clear area. But with the grades and timber there was none of this, so I had to disassemble my equipment somewhat and carry it in portions to a space deep within the timber. Once in there, I found a great spot between several large ponderosa pines. I did not think about it, but because of the tight switchbacks I was actually between folds of the road.

keremeye'us

It meandered in layers above and below me.

That evening I ate early and unexpectedly fell asleep soon after six p.m. At three a.m. I awoke to heavy snows sliding off of my tent. It had snowed several inches, but upon investigation found that I was now between storms. I decided to continue my ascent towards Bridesville as soon as possible. With that, I fired up a small but tremendously powerful gas lantern and hung it from the rickshaw, still inside the tent.

That portion of the Crowsnest Highway is quiet in winter and at three a.m. on a blustery winter's night only the occasional trucker can be found edging his way over the pass. So it was that on this night at the same time as I was starting to pack up my gear, an over-tired and over-worked trucker started his slow descent down from Bridesville. Out of coffee and cranked up on cigarettes and power drinks, and fighting the ice and fog, he struggled to stay awake. In the fog and snow the switchbacks seemed endless and he fought every minute just to stay awake and keep his rig on the pavement.

As he cut back and forth something caught his eye and then it was gone. Again, there in front on him, a glow. Again it was gone. He felt a cold chill creep down his back. Totally alert now, he gulped down the last of the power drink and strained his eyes against a darkness marbled with cloud and reflection of light. There it was again below him, then aloft, moving slowly. He began to freak out. As he abandoned his concern of the road and concentrated on the orange dome hovering in the timber to his right, then his left, he lost all sense of space and then all sense of reason. All those years of listening to late night conspiracy and alien talk shows on the radio fell upon him like a bag of cement and rather than inching down the steep grade, he was now accelerating. The trailer whipped around like a headless serpent, kissing the edges of the ditch, and the driver, convinced that he was going to be transported to the mother ship to be prodded and examined, perhaps his brain removed or worse, lost all composure.

Since the incident at the ravine the past season I had a

healthy respect for personal safety. The words "rollover at four kilometers per hour" made clear that an accident could happen even when walking. So it was with this in mind that, before actually starting to take down the tent and pack up the gear, I wanted to check out the footing and find the safest route back to the road. I had packed my gear up the night before from below, but now I saw that I was between the roads and edged along the ledges, eventually finding myself right at the inside curve of the switchback. It was a decent spot to access the road as just to my right I could easily negotiate the grade. Where I was standing, the tight switchback wrapped around me more than 180 degrees and in relation to the road surface, I was about eight feet above it. It was from this location, with the glowing tent in the timber behind me that I first heard the growl of the engine brakes of a truck far above.

I knew something was wrong immediately as his descent was fractured, at times jamming on the brakes, then speeding up, his headlights moved through the fog wildly and I immediately thought of a runaway. Safe on the inside of the corner, I watched him pinball down the last two switchbacks and swing in one wild attempt to make the curve. He did, but his trailer carved up the shoulder and it nearly rolled. Coming down at an accelerating pace to my left, he was about to enter the second "S" and I could see the horror in his face.

I am sure he was convinced an alien ship was pursuing him. As he bore down upon the wheel and leaned into the turn, he was screaming like a schoolgirl, his dash lights illuminating the dread and panic in his eyes. He did not see me, standing on the rock outcropping, as it was clear his "flight mode" was in full session. Nor did he consider the winding road and grade. Gearing up, the black smoke surged from the pipes as the tractor and trailer skidded in panorama in front of me.

Incredibly, the turn was cleared, and the trailer disappeared into the night below, all the time chasing a higher gear and finally putting distance between him and the alien ship, which had clearly been in pursuit. I often wonder if he told anyone of

keremeye'us

his encounter. Maybe the experience changed his life, perhaps he sold his truck and tried to find his family again; perhaps he turned to God or now occupies a bar stool at some dark tavern near Butte, Montana. Whatever the case, I will never forget his eyes and the sheer terror as he passed in front of me.

After one more night in the heavy snows, I dropped down into the Kettle River Valley and enjoyed a fabulous breakfast at Rock Creek. I was tired, though, as the night before had been filled with commotion. Because of the snows it was hard to find a location to camp. I had waited too long and decided to take up a small space at the end of a wide, well-marked spot in the road reserved for trucks to check their brakes and chain up. There was so little truck traffic and the tent was so visible that I felt it would be safe to stay there. It was safe, the police officer deemed, soon after waking me at one a.m.

The night was chaotic because firstly, I had near one hundred mice slip from under the edges of the snow bank and crawl everywhere on, under, and on top of the tent. Then, it seemed I was in the middle of an owl migration route or convention, each trying to out-hoot each other. Then the mice vanished like a whiff of wind only to be replaced by a pack of playful and horny coyotes, yipping and howling and spooning all about the place. Next, a cranky truck driver who parked inches from the tent and then decided it was time to smash off that rusty, three-inch nut that he had forgotten about. Lastly, two love sick cows, one on the top side of the road and the other below, bellowed all night in a tragic opera of separation. In the morning, I looked like a bag of shit.

I had a few days to recover, though, as I paced along the tranquil Kettle River. I took a local's advice and opted to follow the Kettle River into Washington State. The river flows south over the border and then back into Canada at Grand Forks. The grade is near level as opposed to the snow-covered Eholt Pass on the northern route. It was a smart move and the weather cooperated, and a few days later I arrived back in British Columbia.

I arrived in Grand Forks about mid-day and other than

Joseph Woodcock

an expectation of a feed of pirogy and a bowl of borscht, I had not expected to stay for long. As I shuffled into town, the locals took note and though I was served and treated well, the western mystic of downtown and the bewildered stares from the boardwalks gave me an inclination to move on. Then, there was a terrific screech of tires and out of a car bolts a woman yelling, "Joey, Joey." She was wearing a series of flowing scarfs or robes or a poncho or all of those and a French beret, sort of a Euro-hippy thing. There were beads and hoops, rings on her toes, ankle bracelets, and a beautiful smile. As she bound toward me and then latched onto the entire bonnet of the rickshaw, she gave a great squeeze and let out a type of banshee howl. I was a bit stunned.

Then the answer came to me, and just in time. This was Susan, my elder sister's dear friend and she had expected my arrival and had actually posted a sign west of town to welcome me. But in taking the route through Washington State, I had missed it. Bouncing wildly with excitement, Susan insisted that I spend the night and I was happy to accept. I was going to spend the afternoon in town and then follow her vague description of the route to her place. It was a terrific surprise and I took in a few sights that afternoon before meandering toward the edge of downtown Grand Forks. Of course, the directions were a challenge, but I knew that I was in the right area when I heard yelling and screaming from across a potato field. There was Susan waving her arms and directing me farther along to catch a crossroad back to her home. I was not the only one who heard her, as most of the neighbours, raking their lawns and tending to the flowerbeds, watched me with concern as I slogged along the boulevard.

I was welcomed with open arms and we had a terrific night talking about the past and present. In the morning after a good breakfast, I loaded up my rickshaw and after passing through the town centre again, made my way east toward Christina Lake. For the neighbours, my stay at Susan's was a concern and tantalizing for the local grapevine. Susan had a grown son who worked for the local public works and by chance he had no knowledge of me and had not seen me pass through town. In the morning at the public works garage the crews shared morning coffee and gossip.

Her son listened as the conversation broached the subject of the homeless man, and when it did all eyes seem to turn toward him. There was an uneasy pause as everyone waited for his comment. Confused, he replied with a general statement regarding the plight of the homeless and then went back to his newspaper. The conversation continued regarding the state of the homeless man who paid for his lunch with US currency but gave a generous tip. Some thought he was an undercover border agent as Grand Forks is known for its illicit cultivation and trade in marijuana. Others rejected that and reported that the man was unkept and ranked of body odour, had poor teeth, and suffered from mental illness.

Throughout the morning coffee, eyes kept coming back to Susan's son for comment or reaction and soon he was feeling uneasy with the situation. Finally, after being pried for an opinion regarding the state-sponsored electrocution of the homeless, he snapped back that he did not have an opinion on that or any other thing to do with the homeless man or the mentally ill in general. There was a void and a prolonged vacuum before one of the men cleared his throat and replied, "We were just wondering what you thought because your mother spent the night with that bum."

Susan had heard the phone ring a few times during her shower and then again when she was changing but ignored it until she was in the kitchen, when it rang again. She was taken back with the abruptness of her son's voice, "Where have you been, I have been phoning for thirty minutes?" Susan, sensing a bit of panic in his voice replied that she had been in the shower. "In the shower?" he barked, "That's a minimum, you should get to a clinic and get checked, I mean, Jesus Christ!" Susan fell silent. "I mean, have you no self-esteem? Where is it all going? I mean, you babysit kids, people know you; they know me." And on it went until Susan started to laugh. Although the explanation was good enough for her son, it was the newspaper article the next day in the local paper with my photo and story that officially vindicated her.

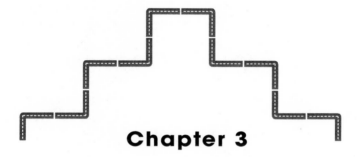

Chapter 3

In the days ahead I camped overlooking frozen Christiana Lake, then took refuge from a wild winter storm somewhere above that, hunkering in my tent for two days and nights. I then slipped between storms to bolt over the Paulson Pass. After almost a week of gruelling travel from Grand Forks in heavy snows, I welcomed a bath and soft bed in Castlegar. I had wondered throughout the past winter as I worked in northern Alberta on the pipeline if I should have continued my walk through the winter. Well, after my week crossing the Paulson Pass, I was content to rule out winter treks. It was not because of the effects of the elements on me personally, but the increase in day-to-day chores.

For one thing, all water had to be converted from snow—a time-consuming process of gathering snow and then melting it in a pot. The temperature was about -18 C, so any water you did not use simply froze. When pulling the rickshaw I would drink about six litres of water per day, and if it was anywhere other than in my jacket it was frozen solid by mid-day. Wet clothes were impossible to dry, so they froze and very soon stove gas was in short supply. Off of the mountains now, in mid-March, the valleys were generally clear of snow and conditions for trekking were good. With the Crowsnest Pass through the Rockies still two weeks away, I welcomed the sight of the Columbia River valley below.

After a couple nights in Castlegar, I moved steadily along the lower reaches of the Kootenay River, first to Nelson and then to Balfour, and was taken in and fed at almost at every turn. The weather was crisp and thin ice still nudged from the secluded bays under the gaze of the Kokanee Glacier. The fresh snow-line etched against the surly green of the peaks, pronounced and finite, defining two vast domains. The waters here, so deep and cold, refuse to relinquish the dead; instead, they express and celebrate their spirits in reflections of radiant blue. Great valleys surrender their bounty, submissively releasing jagged scars of torrent against a gentle, delicate stillness. The people wish you a good day and mean it. In the streets, sandals and smiles abound; arms are opened, not just to welcome, but also to embrace. An invitation, an open door, and shelter from the rain...in the cafes, a chair always awaits you and to walk away, completely away, well, one never can.

After the "longest free ferry ride in the world" across Kootenay Lake, I climbed the undulating grades through Crawford Bay and then south, along the rocky shore. The rain rolled across the open water as a surge, collapsing to soggy burlap upon the slopes. Befriended by the dark canopy of forest, I kept a strong pace through the cascade and as the hours passed, deep within myself, I was thinking of Patrick.

We, as a family, had moved from Revelstoke to the Cowichan Valley when I was seven. Very soon afterward, my brother Mike read me a column in the local newspaper about a naturalist group. The column was penned by a local birdwatcher, Patrick Glascock who, at the end of his article, invited anyone who was interested to join. The very next Saturday morning, at the age of seven, I jumped on my bike with a lunch, a thermos of tea, and my father's weighty binoculars and rode the five kilometers to Somenos Lake.

I arrived at Somenos Lake early and spent the twenty minutes

Joseph Woodcock

watching a man who had binoculars and was watching me too. He was down the dike quite a distance. At first I thought he was the owner of the farm but immediately upon my arrival he abandoned whatever he was doing and monitored my every move. He seemed agitated, at times pacing and with my father's powerful moose-hunting binoculars I could even see the gold in his teeth as he grimaced at me. It was a bit unsettling. His body language seemed to get worse if I walked anywhere in the vicinity of the parked car that was there.

It was a strange car, a large, non-descript sedan, which reminded me of something out of the Dragnet series on television. The small man wore a windbreaker jacket, slacks, and an English-style cap, all in neutral colours, and glasses that he seemed to tear off his face each time he lifted the binoculars to follow my movement. I found him quite peculiar and almost immediately decided that I liked him.

Then in small pods, several Mercedes-Benzes entered the parking lot and out of each one stretched a grey-haired English woman. They immediately began to cackle and honk as if the neighbour's hound had entered the yard. Without taking the time to breathe, the gaggle drowned out the rush of highway traffic, passed each other sweaters, exchanged what could have been recipes for cobbler, and apparently admired each other's Italian walking shoes. Turning quickly to the totty little man on the dike, I saw him looking at the women with his binoculars, his grimace had turned to a look of distain and then scolding himself he quickly swung his stare back to me, as if, for a second, he had let down his guard. Unexpectedly, and I think with some disappointment, the man found that I, in his few seconds of inattention, had not slipped around to flank him nor made off with his car.

It did not seem as though the situation was going to move forward. The ladies were all gathered around in a circle, possibly discussing honeybees, I was standing in the middle of the parking lot, and this potty little man was clearly growing increasingly annoyed at both parties. So, supporting the large set of binoculars around my neck and a satchel my father had in the war, I walked

keremeye'us

up to the circle of women and introduced myself. "Hi, my name is Joey and I am here for the birds." Immediately and overwhelmingly the women adopted me and within seconds, it seemed, I was juggling a selection of cookies and cakes.

Each of the ladies had at least one turn in pinching my cheeks and with all of the excitement and attention, I briefly forgot about the man on the dike. He did not forget me though, as I saw him enter the parking lot and quickly inspect his car for damage or signs of forced entry. He then came over to the group who quickly swatted at their slacks and nonchalantly preened their appearance before, in unison, wishing Patrick good morning. He continued to look annoyed and impatient, but managed a plastic and shallow smile as if he was feeling the early onset of a toothache.

The women abandoned me first in singles and then as a group to hear his plans for the day. It was like he was reading an eviction notice but the ladies delighted in his every word. As Patrick read out the list of locations and in which order, the ladies, in a growing applause, excitedly repeated his words. "Oh...oh, the sewage lagoons, I hope we see a green heron!" Again, hoots and ovation as Patrick barely mouthed the words "mud flats."

There was some bustling about over who was going to go with whom and if hairnets or umbrellas were needed. The women fell about each other not wanting to be the last to leave. Patrick was already three-quarters of the way to his car when I passed him and stood by the passenger's door. I had never, ever experienced a locked car door before, but something told me that this one was locked and I stood dutiful and erect. Patrick assumed I would travel with the womenfolk and was visibly taken off guard with my eagerness to ride with him. I did not look directly at him, but watched him gaping at me from the corner of my eye. He made a few attempts to talk, stepping forward and assuming a stance that could have been that of a confused and deprived victim. Then he swung about in dismay and showed signs of panic as, one by one, the small diesel motors clattered to life. Patrick's greatest fear of not being the first car out read like a death warrant on his face.

Nearly airborne, Patrick scrambled into the driver's seat. I *had noticed but was not shocked to see the door unlock remotely, a rare feature back then. The car had tinted, electric windows that operated at high speed and zipped down as we entered the busy highway. The car pounced from a near static position to highway speed in just a few seconds as we entered the bumper-to-bumper traffic. Then like a guillotine, the windows sliced upward and sealed off the sound of screeching tires as I was pushed back onto the leather seat. There was no gap in the traffic so Patrick made one through both lanes and instantly peeled up against the rear of a station wagon as if he was about to bump it and the family, into the lake.*

Banging on the dash Patrick yelled, "Bastard. You God damn bastard," and then inched first into the oncoming traffic and then to the ditch in an attempt to pass. There were no seat belts in those days so I tried, without touching anything, to sit composed as Patrick barked and threatened everyone and everything on the road. Along with the features I mentioned, the car had twice as much power as my father's Dodge 440 station wagon, and though it was quite new, it had no markings or chrome of any kind. There was no make, model, or any identifiable features. I felt like I was birdwatching with a federal agent.

It would be another total book to detail our friendship. Patrick and I spent nearly every Saturday together for the next eight years. I honestly know little of Patrick; he said he was born in Wales and had an engineering background, a bachelor with no children. He talked little of his past, nothing, in fact. But for years we hiked the mountains, slogged through tidal flats and inched along every creek and river in search of birds. Generally cranky and disapproving, Patrick also had a delightful sense of humour.

One Saturday morning we roared into a sideways stop at a local pullout to search for a Western wood peewee. Patrick had left the ladies far behind in traffic and he was eager to put some walking distance between them and us as quickly as possible. Patrick shrieked at me, now about eight years old, to bring the spotting scope and of course, everything and anything else associated with, or related to, a successful and provable sighting of the species.

keremeye'us

Of course, we knew there was no Western wood peewee. As Patrick put it, "some shut-in with an oversized bib" claimed she saw a Western wood peewee at the institution's bird feeder and to appease her, her daughter, sourcing a field guide, described the sighting to the Provincial Museum and, quite excited, they phoned Patrick. Patrick said to me that she "probably saw a balloon animal."

Regardless, as I rushed to catch up to Patrick along the gravel road, laden heavy with equipment, a snipe flew out from below Patrick's feet at the edge of the road. The snipe is known for darting out at the last second and almost without fail, after several circles, will land in the exact same spot. So it was this day as the snipe kept rank and fell back into the duff under the edge of the road.

I was still trying to attain the impossible task of being able to exit the car at the same time as Patrick, run to the back and match the speed of the electronic trunk release, unlatch and extend the legs of a tripod and spotting scope, load up two lunches, one camera bag with lenses, seasonal clothing, field guides, a folding chair, and a flask of Patrick's tea and then make up the distance between the car and a speed-walking Patrick without running or in any way "compromising the opportunity," as Patrick portrayed it.

Patrick took on behaviour as though we were on stage immediately after exiting the car; he had perfected a set of physical rules that projected complete neutrality to the audience. This included a steady pace, free of any arm waving, and no conversation. A soft step, but no lurking. No protruding objects that could be conveyed as a weapon or worse, a concealed weapon. Eyes were straight ahead and slightly downward, a straight back, slightly leaning forward to project a continued and predictable exit, and finally, no rubbing or abrasion of any unnatural fabric, especially anything petroleum-based such a vinyl or polyester.

Already perspiring from the tension and predicted failure of meeting these expectations, I stumbled under the burden of the equipment. Concentrating on what Patrick would require once and if he did stop, I ran through the process of how I would dismantle the packs and set up the equipment with military speed and precision. Patrick, for the most part would not look for birds, but rather listen and then, once detected, he may insert a physical pause in reacting to the call, a delay that, as he would say, "... lulls the bird into a sense of unimportance and therefore turns their attention to other possible threats."

The pause itself was a model of operatic detail as the group could not just stop; the strides had to be slowed and controlled like a freight train rolling to an eventual and prolonged static condition. At times, the women were stretched out over the mountain trails like members of the ill-fated Donner party, dishevelled and exhausted. As the ladies made their way to where we were standing silently, each broke into a choreographic flamingo-type step for the last few meters.

This kind of shit went on and on and by the end of the day, we all hated each other. I would slam the door and Patrick would screech off, no one would say goodbye to each other. You were just disgusted with yourself for the first few days, but by mid-week you were laughing about it and by Friday the anticipation of what that lunatic was going to do next was just too much miss.

I almost ran right into Patrick as he had turned and was walking back toward the car. Slightly confused, I continued to walk a bit more, looking back at Patrick as he meandered, hands clasped behind his back, to the parking area. Then he stopped and just stood there; he seemed to be waiting for the ladies to arrive. I had never seen this and slowly edged in his direction until I was nearby. Patrick, in a calm voice, asked if I had his tea and after groping around in a few circles like a dog chasing his tail, I pulled out the flask of tea and gave it to him. By now the grey and dusty-blue Mercedes were shuffling into the lot—the ladies were also visibly taken by Patrick waiting patiently for them.

It was a happy surprise and they bubbled with glee as Patrick waved them in one-by-one to the circle. He was drinking his cup of tea and actually chatting with a couple of the ladies regarding the "dreadful scourge of aphids" this year that had fallen upon his strawberries. I stood there frozen, everything seemed lop-sided, not quite together as Patrick passed me back the thermos and thanked me. He then was about to start walking when he turned back and, like a minister, gave a wondrous and sincere sermon of gratitude to what we were about to share. With open arms and a wide smile, his gold caps glistening in the morning sun, Patrick praised and welcomed the natural bounties about and in one last discourse, strung the final two stanzas together as musical and whimsical lyrics.

I thought a few of the ladies were going to collapse as the performance would have been mystic and magical if conducted in a grand music or opera hall complete with a symphony, lights, and an astounding set, but Patrick enchanted and inspired the group to the edge of tears on a wide spot in the road, strewn with garbage and smelling of wet upholstery. "Let us walk," he motioned as the group fell in behind him in reverence. I was last and still having trouble getting past Patrick thanking me for the tea, never mind trying to digest the tranquil and delicate oration he presented.

Still trying to piece together the events, I caught myself callously walking without displaying complete neutrality and quickly fell into line. But Patrick encouraged the ladies to move about him and as they neared the edge of the road, he softly signalled for the group to freeze. It was not one of his normal commando raid-like gestures, but a pope-like open palm request for calm; I was dismayed. Once the group was silent and still, Patrick began to lurk forward in long, dodging strides and he instantly reminded me of the wolf approaching the cottage in Little Red Riding Hood. The ladies though, still swooning with emotion, missed the contradictions and froze in eager anticipation. Patrick whispered back to the group that he could "smell a snipe" and slightly lifted his head to catch the soft breeze. He then stepped to and fro until he zeroed in on the clump of grass at the end of the road. Hesitating, and then with a quick jolt, he clapped his hands and, bursting from the duff, a snipe bounded upward, calling out in sharp cries of disapproval.

In unison, the ladies collapsed back in disbelief, staggered, and each reached out to one another for physical support. An aberration, a gift, a sign—the ladies swelled with celestial enthusiasm as Patrick continued to hold the crouched pose. With effect somewhere between the final seconds of an Elvis Presley ballad

Joseph Woodcock

and a sermon that had just evangelically delivered the will of God, Patrick vibrated and shimmied, his face red and drawn. I think he was actually looking for laughter, but the ladies surged forward, swarming him with accolades. Helping him to his feet, the ladies scurried to brush him off and pat from his cheeks and brow a few small beads of sweat.

He was a clearly uncomfortable with the initial result but he never rejected or promoted the event and allowed the legend to simmer. Of those who witnessed it, some later discounted it as a stunt and some quietly believed what they saw. The miracle was never repeated and as for Patrick and I, it was never acknowledged other than an initial passing smile and twinkle of gold.

Arriving in Boswell in the late afternoon, I began to stretch out my tent poles in the parking lot of a small park. The rain had not let up all day and, under the bulk of the climax forest, the light grew feeble and dim. A car slid in through the open gate and without hesitation, I was invited into the driver's family home for the evening. I accepted and threw the tent back in its bag and humped up the hillside and steep drive to a hot shower and soft bed. Already appreciative, I was later produced as a guest at the local community hall for a St. Patrick's Day potluck dinner. That evening I enjoyed friendly conversation and, bloated with great food, took in the warmth and kindness of the community.

The next day was another wet and windy one, ending at a local pub. Totally soaked, I was enjoying a hot coffee and the daily special when I was invited to take up shelter in a family's travel trailer in Wynndel, a few kilometers farther down the road. When I arrived, everything I carried was soaked so, just after six in the evening, I hung up what I could in the warmth of the caravan and fell into a deep and peaceful sleep.

By morning, with the storm passed, I walked the ten or so kilometers to the town of Creston and since I once lived there, spent a couple of days reminiscing and visiting old friends. It is a peaceful place of apple blossoms and temperate winds—a retirement location for many folk seeking shelter from the

keremeye'us

harsh winter climate of the prairies. Noted for its slow pace, Creston also does not recognize any time change throughout the year and as I sat on the curb at the local gas station talking with a group of local youth, one of them commented, "It is so boring here, nothing ever changes, not even the time."

Kitten and I, along with our two children, had once lived in a small cottage south of Creston in the woods near the US Border. As usual, the situation was not Kitten's idea and far from her first choice. But I had coaxed and needled her until she agreed to go. We had the land but little else and for a few thousand dollars we built a cottage, so to speak, overlooking the Kootenay River as it flowed back into Canada from the Idaho panhandle.

I had no real completion schedule, so we lived in a tent inside the shell of the cottage and Kitten would bathe herself and the kids in the frigid Goat River. It was another one of my dreams, not hers, but come winter with only a wood stove for heat and miles from town, I was temporarily transferred to another work location. It was a temporary posting, so I stayed in a hotel with free food, satellite TV, and all the comforts.

Kitten, on the other hand, spent most of the winter snowed in with two small children, having to chop wood, unfreeze water lines, and deal with a porta-potty that weighed one hundred pounds when full. At night coyotes howled in the woods at the edge of the clearing, snapping and gnawing at the scents, the dim porch light offering little deterrence to their nightly visits. Our dog, Muffy, whom I touted as the protector while I was away, would sleep on the couch on his back with his paws in the air and one of those large dog smiles and not even hear Kitten stumble down the stairs three times a night to stoke the fire. She would venture out onto the porch and carry in wood laden with snow and ice and then, crashing all about, fill the stove and slam the door. All this and Muffy may let out a small sigh or perhaps one paw would twitch.

We also had a cow, which we named Burger just to set straight our intentions. Burger had some thyroid or hormone thing going on and generally ran all the time. Of course, when he ran the dog ran, too, so most of the day they ran. I think this was the main reason Muffy slept so soundly. Burger could leap fences at will and ate every flower Kitten ever planted.

One day while our son Michael was playing in some dirt with a small car, Burger and Muffy were doing wind sprints and, without warning, Burger started to run at full speed toward our son. Kitten started screaming, but there was no opportunity to get there in time as Burger bore down on the three-year-old. As Burger ran by in a full gallop, he softly picked up the toy car in his mouth and continued to run around the yard with Michael screaming for his toy. Everyone was yelling, but Burger flipped the toy in the air and dropped playfully a few times, each time picking it up again and dodging our attempts to corral him.

I knew then his days were numbered, but my intentions of feeding the family on him were unrealistic, as Burger had no meat on him and resembled a ripped weightlifter. When his day finally did come, the butcher had no success in throwing a rope on him and soon became exhausted. Finally, after pulling out his rifle, the butcher said Burger had displayed mocking gestures and managed to sidestep the first two rounds. Instead of filling the freezer, we got a bill in the mail.

Walking out of Creston in the early morning, I crossed the Goat River and then spent a night in Yahk and then another along the frozen shores of Moyie Lake. The weather had cooled again, but the trekking was calm and I travelled under sporadic light snows and graphite skies. I took advantage of the few quiet pubs along the way for lunch. The comfortable few days brought back memories of working in this area.

While in living in Creston, I worked for a small lumber mill. We were a backwater, so to speak, to the other large and efficient sister mills to the north. Our purpose at the time was to supply some very local employment such that the entire company could share in the timber supply of the area. In general, we handled the off-species and marginal products allowing the larger operations to concentrate on a diet of spruce/pine/fir, or SPF as it is known.

The situation was also hugely political because at the time the Creston operation and timberlands fell within a left-leaning

provincial party and all the other plants and forestlands, includ-
ing Head Office, were in the ridings of the inversely minded right-
wing ridings. I think the expectation was that we had to be a profit
centre; failing in that, we had more laughs than we deserved.

At the head of this operation was our director, Hamish
Inksetter, a large, bloated Scottish man who chain-smoke menthol
cigarettes and drank to excess. Hamish was heavily involved in the
shadows of local politics and several service organisations. Hamish
recognized few rules and was an "ends justifies the means" type
of person, and the "means" always seemed to involve some sort
of clandestine cash from various slush funds. But to his credit,
Hamish was able to balance and extend the life of the money-losing
operation far beyond its useful years of service.

On the flip side, the sister plants were under the tight grip of
Willem Van Oosten, an impatient and stubborn Dutchman who
seethed at Creston's ability to remain operating in the face of con-
tinued losses. Both Hamish and Van Oosten reported directly to
Serge Marshall, a vice president with an engineering background
and degrees and credentials from prestigious universities. No one
could be more opposite of Serge than Hamish, but Serge seemed to
find considerable pleasure in Hamish's non-conventional ability to
sway local leaders into extending already expired agreements and
contracts. Serge also liked a good laugh and story and there was no
one better at this than Hamish.

Hamish would go to extraordinary lengths to sow seeds and
manufacture situations that eventually benefited the Creston
plant, which actually meant they benefited him. This patience and
planning also extended to his incredible sense of humour and sto-
rytelling abilities. Hamish had been asked to speak at a dinner in
Nelson for a long-term manager who was retiring. The manager
was of Yugoslavian origin and Hamish had always taunted him
about that fact, but in the now-prevalent environment of political
correctness, Hamish was persuaded softly by human resources to
dampen his insensitive remarks.

I picked Hamish up a few hours before dinner and we started
the drive to Nelson; of course Hamish was drunk, but somewhat

sombre and quiet. Hamish always looked like he was far past his expiry date and, like every other day I knew him, I was resigned that this was his last and prepared myself for the phone call I would have to make to his family regarding his passing.

Once at the dinner Hamish moped about the place and took long silent minutes just staring at inanimate objects. Normally on the piano by now, or making a pass at some vice president's wife, Hamish's state of mind was noted by everyone and at one point, he was quietly asked if he still wanted to do a speech. Hamish shrugged and rubbed his forehead acknowledging his desire to "set the record straight" and "apologise for his harsh treatment" of the guest of honour for so many years.

Once on stage Hamish crept through their early years together at times stopping to fight back the tears and swallow hard upon chosen words of hardship together. The crowd, of whom many were relatives and family members, some travelling all the way from the old country just for this occasion, wept in Hamish's acknowledgment of the historical hardships and loss and the guest of honour's pride in his family and cultural roots. It was an ovation to the entire life of this man, his family, and the Yugoslavian people—the audience burst with pride, at times humming the anthem of the crumbling nation.

Then Hamish began to broach the caverns of his own racial insensitivity, explaining tearfully and physically reaching out to the head table. He questioned the origins of his ethnic tactlessness with boyhood accounts of life in the coal towns under the yoke of the British master. Hamish was able to promote himself as a victim of his childhood and environment, one trying desperately to shed, apologise and mend the past. Like a truth commission, Hamish sought to unburden himself and finally set himself free. It was a gripping speech, one that threw the audience into open wails of remorse and personal pleas of compassion and forgiveness. I know I was crying and think I was holding Willem's hand; even the staff preparing and serving the meals consoled each other in the hallways and the members of the head table simply came apart.

After several minutes of hugging, promises to each other of

keremeye'us

meaningful and lasting friendships and the discarding of old divisions, Hamish managed to get himself and the packed hall back in some sort of order. He was trying to smile now, the edges of his mouth twitching upward as he spoke of a new day of new hope and renewal. "I mean," he said, "There is still hope for Yugoslavia. Things are improving—technology and innovation are the strength of its past and sure to propel it forward. I mean, look at the wee Lada, a brilliant little car. And just the other day I was reading a newspaper article saying that Yugoslavia had opened a plant to build five thousand septic tanks a year." There was a long pause and then Hamish continued. "Yes, five thousand septic tanks a year and as soon as they find a way to start them they are going to invade Russia."

It was as if every person in the hall was propped up and punched in the stomach. The expulsion of air bowed the walls outward as Hamish drummed through ridiculing tales and jokes regarding anything and everything eastern European. It did not matter if it was historically or geographically inaccurate, or broached the already ultra-sensitive matters of expulsion and cleansing. Hamish, now smoking away, slamming down glasses of Scotch and barked out a steady stream of insulting and demeaning jokes.

The entire human resources department edged closer to him and I think they wished they had a net. Hamish, in seeing the "hyenas," stood on the base on the microphone and gripped the stand. As the master of ceremonies and his "dogs" struggled to pull him off the stage, Hamish continued his barrage and just before someone pulled the cord from the amplifier, Hamish broke into the song Don't cry for me Argentina, which had nothing to do with Eastern Europe, but Hamish liked it.

Someone who did not know Hamish would be surprised to find he still had a job at a minimum, but Hamish could deflect and stumble his way out every situation. Each month, while I worked in Creston, Hamish and I were required to attend a management meeting at the head office. It was generally a bloodbath as all attending had alliances and detractors and the company had a large and efficient accounting and purchasing departments. These departments set the day-to-day rules concerning expenditures and followed up with continuous audit regimes; if you or your departments wavered from these rules you were brought to task and shamed.

Hamish was not much of one for conventions and truly liked the term "general revenue." He tried to slip the phrase in with every conversation he had with anyone who worked in what he called "the head." Hamish and I were never on time for one of these meetings, a fact that infuriated the VP, Serge Marshall. There was always some reason why we could not arrive on time and Hamish always included me as a backup witness.

One early morning I arrived in front of Hamish's house to pick him up for the monthly meeting. Of course, the lights were still out and once inside I found him asleep on his couch with his arms around a stuffed coyote. It was clear he had been hammering on his keyboard and drinking to the early hours of the morning and had finally just fallen over with and cuddled up with Snider. Snider was some mange old coyote that he or one of his drunk friends ran over on the way back from some convention. Hamish had it stuffed in an aggressive manner with teeth bared and normally placed it in front of the basement beer fridge. He took enormous pleasure when he was entertaining new guests to ask one to get a beer from the basement fridge. As the person struggled in the dark to find the fridge, they would either bump into Snider or worse, open the fridge and have its light illuminate the snarl placed permanently on its face. It was one of Hamish's greatest joys.

Once I roused Hamish, I explained in simple language the urgency of him getting dressed and cleaned up and that we could not be late again. I waited in the truck for forty-five minutes, trying to convince myself that it did not matter to me if we were late and that I was doing my best. When Hamish did walk down the path he looked exactly like I had left him on the couch. He was wearing an old pair of running shoes, oversized black track pants with the string hanging out the front and a dirty old T-shirt which exposed part of his belly. His face was creased with the couch zippers, a *crusty white film ran from the corner of his mouth to his ear and his hair was matted to the side of his skull. In the forty-five minutes that I waited, he had only managed to add an oversized scarf that he won as a door prize at the Christmas party. Lighting a cigarette and then scratching his crotch, Hamish slid into the truck and we headed for the meeting.*

Instantly he fell back asleep and remained that way, his head glued to the window, until we turned north on the main highway. At this time, I stopped to get him a coffee at a gas station and Hamish commented on the trucks heading south, carrying lumber from our sister mills to the US. Then as each kilometer passed, Hamish drank his coffee and started to come back to life. At the top of the conversation was the colour of the lumber wrap from the other company mills that had changed from a few deer standing against a white background to the same deer against a urine-yellow background.

The colour was dreadful and the sales and marketing guys were getting ridiculed relentlessly by customers and agents for the change, especially the choice of this yellow. But it had not been because of a marketing study that the colour changed. No one actually knows why, but Willem Van Oosten, probably in playing with his box of candies, decided he liked the colour yellow best and placed an order for a company-wide change to the suppliers. The lumber wrap order was epic and when truckloads of the wrap started arriving at the plants, the phone lines lit up. But Willem simply would not budge and reaffirmed his order to use the yellow wrap as the white ran out. It was a major blunder but Willem wielded almost ultimate power on the manufacturing side and no one would openly oppose or question him, though an underlying fire roared within the different departments within "the head."

When Hamish and I arrived in the parking lot we were only thirty minutes late, which was better than I had expected. What I did not expect was that there was a notable guest at the meeting that day and that Serge had threatened to fire Hamish if he was late. Serge was out of sorts as our parent company from Asia had sent over an observer and the tiny man wanted to sit in on the managers' meeting. Hamish knew this as Serge had related it to him for weeks, but it made no matter.

I quickly slinked into the meeting to the cold stare of Serge and took the first available seat. Hamish, on the other hand, flirted and joked with the girls for some time at the reception desk in clear view of the board room and then found himself a coffee and a Danish before stopping back at the reception desk and then finally stepping into the meeting, which was already in progress. Serge was visibly furious; his face and jowls glowed bright red like he had just drunk a cup of hot sauce, and his small mustache flipped from side to side like a dancing giant beetle. Hamish wished everyone a good morning and introduced himself to our Asian guest. Hamish had totally forgotten his name so just rolled out something like "Nice to meet you Mr. Spaghetti Sun Bologna" and gave him a bit of a hug.

Serge lost composure and started to shout at Hamish regarding him being late again. It was extremely unconventional and uncomfortable as Serge threw out a barrage of loaded questions and even Hamish's detractors could only look at their feet. Hamish looked taken aback but managed a few small bites of his Danish as Serge quickly calmed down and gained some self-control. Then Hamish took a chair and apologized for being late but said it was unavoidable.

That sent Serge off again for a few seconds. It was clear that any rope Serge had given Hamish was at its end, but Hamish, looking a bit dejected, replied, "Joe and I went to bed with the chickens and rose in lots of time to get to the meeting safely. But, when we turned north on the highway and met the line of lumber trucks heading south with that piss-yellow lumber wrap, we had to stop every mile and puke our guts out." The meeting erupted in laughter at first and then all order crumbled as weeks of unspoken tension and disagreement concerning the colour scheme spilled out, hijacking the preapproved but now abandoned agenda.

Hamish also used the managers' meetings to move issues forward inch-by-inch over months and was a master at pitting one against another and exploiting any gaffs or opportunities available—even mine. Prior to Kitten somewhat agreeing to move to the

keremeye'us

bush to live in a small shack, I was pushing for our family just to live in a large tent. Kitten, who was just then starting to realize who or what she had married, and with two young children, was utterly distraught, isolated and sick with worry. The company I worked for was owned by a mammoth Asian conglomerate and as such passed down management philosophy. The first was an Employee and Family Assistance Program which actually was an internal support system to help families with any sort of problems, such as mental illness.

After proposing to Kitten the tent idea she contacted the Family Assistance department and a machine went into motion. Of course, the entire thing is confidential so I would guess only a select few in the company knew I was going mad, including the VP, members of the HR department, and certainly Hamish. Of course, I knew nothing of this. A plan was constructed with Hamish as the main architect—given time and some "support", I may pull out of it. So started the good times for Hamish.

A few days before the managers' meeting Hamish pulled me in and said that I should "be the tip of the sword" on a few Creston initiatives and that he was impressed with me and so on. Although quite taken, I was even more pleased when I saw the official agenda with several brave bullet points after my name. Just to get on the official agenda was difficult as this was often the only window of opportunity to have all company managers and VPs hear any of your ideas. I did not truly know the detail regarding the initiatives, but Hamish gave me some talking points and took me to lunch at the local hotel.

Of course, these initiatives were new only to me, and Willem had pounced upon Hamish months earlier regarding his proposed theft of raw material and had set up a series of well-constructed fire walls which included support and backing from just about every other department and division. Willem was overjoyed that "Hamish's lackey" was going to try and convince the VP for support and overjoyed at the opportunity to dress me down. The meetings were chaired by the VP and as there was no vote on issues discussed it was up to Serge's discretion to move forward or not.

But to the side of the room sat Pierce, the HR VP who always made eye contact with Serge on discussions of anything.

Hamish would say that Pierce's position was really internal, as he had access to all information and the ears of the company president and our Asian handlers. It was a sort of Watergate situation—there was nothing written down and everyone at that level had "plausible deniability" if things ever went south; a raised eyebrow from Pierce on an issue that seemed to have the validity and inertia to move forward would be instantly quashed by Serge with no explanation. But it worked in reverse also, and Hamish knew this well.

In the background Hamish had been waxing the floor regarding my mental state; we went out for lunch every day, purchased a water cooler for his office, and bought a bunch of liquor for a retirement party that never made it there. All of this going on my expense account and quickly approved under the guise of "supporting Joe." So it was that when I read out the Creston initiatives under the mocking and hungry glare of Willem that Serge instantly sanctioned the transfers with no discussion. It was a monetarily neutral move for the company as a whole, but for Willem, it plucked away several higher margin production processes. Dumbfounded, Willem began to stammer but was cut off by the glare of Serge who simply replied, "We have moved on; next item."

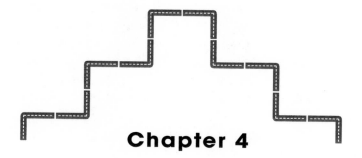

Chapter 4

Camping on the edge of Cranbrook, I took an opportunity to buy some supplies and then in the mid-morning made my way through the small city and stopped for coffee. As I rearranged my fresh supplies, a large crowd inside watched my every move until I entered. Then, after fielding questions for a few minutes, I ended up at the counter before the bright smile of a young lady. Before she could take my order a lanky store manager bumped her out of the way and asked what I would like.

As the elderly crowd looked on from the tables, I received my coffee and muffins and then began to count through my change to make payment. Stopping me, and in a loud clear voice, the manager insisted, "This is on the house," and thanked me for my work. A little confused, I stood there pondering the phrase "for my work" when the young man asked me what "cause" I was walking for. I replied that there was "no cause... just because" and we looked at each other for a few long seconds. As it sunk in, the manager realized that I was supporting no one and I followed his eyes to the two muffins on the plate. I thought he was going try and grab them back, so I quickly licked both of them, thanked him very much and took a place near the window.

That evening I camped on the banks of the Kootenay River across from the settlement of Wardner, then again near Elko and, taking advantage of the slight grades, pushed through to enjoy a room in Fernie. Stretching out under light snows, any fatigue was lost to the weeks behind me and I edged along the Elk River, now thinking of the Crowsnest Summit ahead and my first significant milestone, the British Columbia–Alberta Border. As I enjoyed a cup of tea and a biscuit at roadside, a simple small car passed and out of its window stuck the smiling face of a white bull terrier. The terrier watched me until the small car disappeared into the shadow of the rock tunnel. Its grin expressed true happiness with the day and took me back to our home in the Cowichan Valley.

At the end of our road, hidden in the heavy conifers, was the municipal pound. The operator was a sleek and wily Englishman by the name of Donald Smyth. Don operated the pound as a business first, though he was a lover of all and anything that could be domesticated. Beside Patrick's bi-weekly newspaper article on birds was Don's witty and smart column on pets. Don owned many animals personally and two of these were white bull terriers.

A few years after we moved to the Cowichan Valley our dog Blackie disappeared and we all presumed he had slipped away to die somewhere. With this, we went without a dog for several years, though I still had chickens, ducks, and some cheeky budgies. But a boy in the country without a dog is at a loss and at age ten I asked my father for another. He directed me to go visit Don and see what he could do. So I approached Don and somewhere in the kennels found a black and white spaniel whom I named Oscar. No money changed hands, but Don required twenty hours of work as payment.

So each day for a week I struggled under the hot sun cleaning kennels and dragging brush around trying to complete the deal. The work was hard and Don was extremely specific on hours of work, what had to be done, and by when. Also, Don had a strange way about him, I thought. Sometimes I would see him standing

Joseph Woodcock

off to one side, supporting a cigarette holder or cigarillo, with a glassy smile as if he was enjoying the deal just too much. I think he liked the idea of indentured child labour but there seemed to be more and I grew wary. I could not wrap my head around it, but, for instance, each time I required a drink of water and wrapped my mouth around the water hose nozzle, there was Don, smiling as a fox and egging me to "Drink up Joey...yes, the sun is hot."

I had known Don for years and knew he loved a good joke, especially a well-constructed one, but I had no idea at the time that one was in progress. A few days later I completed my required hours and Don allowed me to take Oscar home. In leaving, Don became very appreciative of my work and thanked me for the few extras I had included. He had only one suggestion though and took me into a dirty kennel with dog feces scattered about the concrete pen. He showed me with the hose, the only one in the facility, that when he cleans the pens and comes to piles of excrement that are hard to remove, he scrapes them off with the nozzle.

Then in slow stroking movements with a devious smile upon his face, he pushed and drew the water nozzle through the shit until it lifted. "Like this, let the nozzle do the work," he beamed as I held my stomach and sat on the bench. "Like this Joey, right through the shit," he continued, almost bursting with glee at the sight of my fading condition. Arriving home in tears, embarrassed and ashamed, I told my mother what he had done. She did not go straight down there or phone the municipal office or local news-paper, neither the health board nor clinic were summoned but my mother in response to her son digesting dog shit, expressed her dissatisfaction by shouting, "Those bloody English!" And then she went back to her book.

In the last few days of March I left the banks of the Elk River and began the climb to the Crowsnest Summit. Although the weather had been fine, I spent an extra night in the valley and enjoyed the solitude. I camped in the standing timber beside a small creek. I had a tarp and built a small sweat lodge using my camp stove and a pot of boiling water. So that evening, I went back and forth from the frozen edges of the creek to the relative warmth of the lodge in the darkness of the timber, only the partial moon as my guide. My body numbed to the difference and finally I slipped into the tent and sipping a cup of tea, collapsed into sleep. The last week had been a good one for walking and I was thankful that the Elk River cut so far into the mountains without any steep grades. Now as I had done before with the other mountain passes, I would try to burst up the last grades and find shelter early in the day.

Leaving Sparwood in the darkness, I pulled upward through the winding highway under wet snows. The surface was bare so when I could I stretched out the pace and felt my lungs struggle against the altitude and burden of the load. In the clouds and as the hours passed I lost my sense of distance and concentrated on moving upward. With the twists and turns it was difficult to predict the next hour and even though I was soaked with sweat and craved a hot bowl of soup, I was vulnerable if the weather got worse. In the early afternoon the snows, which were now lighter, drifted upward alongside of me on the currents surging through the passes ahead. Motivated, I trotted through the borderless whites and greys, now withdrawn and introverted as the winds cut into my wet skin and crept along my spine. Then, without pomp, a turnout in the road appeared and a small sign marked the summit.

As soon as I stopped walking I began to shake. The winds now lifted and shook the rickshaw and crusted snow and ice hung like a carcass upon my equipment. I made myself ignore all of this and set up the camera and took a photo of myself and the rickshaw against the backdrop of the sign marking the summit. With the click of the shutter I rushed to store everything back and then stepped into the province of Alberta now looking for any spot flat enough to set up my tent and spend the night. The prevailing Pacific winds, compressed and caged, pushed me as a cork through the white-out until I found a level piece of ground on which to camp.

Rushing to pin down the tent against the storm I fell inside and lay for a quiet minute. I lay there silently on the floor of the tent, my hands and feet numb, and listened to the surge of the storm lash against the walls of the tent. The temperature was falling and the traffic, which had rolled past me exposing stark gazes of disbelief, grew silent. Within minutes the orange of the tent slipped into the snow and ice and then, as a mirage, became one with the surroundings. In the hours ahead, as the definition and detail vanished, I sat back, read my maps, and looking forward, celebrated with a cup of coffee.

The storm lasted throughout the night and well into the next day and even though I had no real choice, I was content to read my book and relax for another night at the summit. By late evening of the second day it was clear that the spring storm was over and I walked to a nearby rise to watch the stars glisten against the darkness. The crust of snow, ten feet deep on the leeward side of the crest, was slight and faint against the westward rise of the slope and I walked easily several hundred feet in elevation with only the carpet of stars and a shy, partial moon as my chaperone.

As I had slept off and on during the day, I was not tired and now, supporting dry clothes, I crouched under some shrubs, which were bent nearly to the ground by the constant winds. For a few hours I sat there, looking eastward, dwarfed under the silent, still peaks of the pass. It was a drug, digital and crisp, the gentle rotation of the sky against the jagged outline of the peaks and within, a soft warmth. It was a time and place that one should have looked deep within and made peace with oneself, and perhaps God; I just could not take away my eyes nor fail to appreciate each breath.

The wind, now delicate, sifted snow as fine as sand over the edges of the ridgeline and its motion, as silk against the skin, drew a tender shiver along my spine. Modest to their influence, the spirits slipped around me and swam in the soft, flowing currents of the night as far below, and even farther away the mortal and the meek slept safe and warm. So silent and benign was the darkness, and so distant my fears, that I felt a gentle embrace and was solaced by the beauty. As distant sirens, their

keremeye'us

songs faint and lost, the gentle tide carried me away and for a time, I was aloft, it seems.

I awoke in the morning to crystal blue skies. The glare, walking into the rising sun against the genteel white of the valley, was an abrupt contrast to the night before. Although the radiant warmth was so welcome, the morning seemed noisy in comparison to the soft silence of the ridgeline. For most of the day, though, each time I looked back, the jagged peaks that mark the pass and on whose lower ridges I had walked remained visible, as though we held a quiet secret together.

As the day drew on I passed through the Municipality of Crowsnest Pass and enjoyed both a late breakfast and coffees in the restaurants along the way. Past the Frank Slide I camped on the side of the highway in the early evening after a great day of walking. The sky had not changed all day and I had picked up some pieces of firewood along the road. As the valley opened up to the foothills I sat and toasted my dinner as a cowboy might, among the sparse grassland and distant howl of coyotes. I felt so fortunate that evening and thought back to the times when I had little.

I had been working in northern Alberta and living in my 1982 Volvo. I had converted the sedan to my living quarters for a period of eight months from September to April and travelled about the province and into the Northwest Territories doing short-term work. I had built a bed on the passenger side of the car which stretched from the dashboard to the rear window. This allowed me access to the back seat, but the best feature was that once lying on my back, I was able to look upward through the sloping windshield and watch the northern lights. I had made my kitchen in the trunk so that when opened I could operate my gas stove and wash dishes.

But any dream has its moments and I had run into a company who would not pay me for my work and thus left me in a tough situation. I had quickly secured some other work but would not get paid for several weeks, so soon I ran out of gas money and then out of food. I had taken to leaving the car parked in town and walking the railway tracks to the sawmill about ten kilometers away. My

Joseph Woodcock

shifts were ten hours long and then generally some overtime so by the time I got back to the car, I was done. But day in and day out I slogged back and forth, living on peanut butter and those packaged noodle soups. Finally, with that exhausted, I ate whatever I had until Thursday night.

I was to get paid Friday morning, so I looked at what money I had on hand and with that, pooled together with the money from some bottles I had found, was able to buy a couple bulk hamburger buns and two thick meat ends from the deli. I knew I had some mustard in the car and I had taken a few tea bags from the lunch-room at work, so I was so excited to sit down with a cup of tea and two baloney sandwiches. I had to be careful, though, as the local peace officers were terrorizing me for living in my car. I had made the distinction that I was just sleeping in my car, not cooking and, as such, was not really living in it. This gave me a bit of time, but I am sure if they saw the kitchenette in the trunk it would be hard to explain.

Once back at the car I placed my bit of small meat ends on the top of the car and flipped open the trunk to make tea and prepare the sandwich. All excited and a bit jittery from lack of nourishment, I clambered around trying to get things in order. As I spread the mustard on the buns I looked for the meat ends and after a few seconds of panic remembered I had placed them on the roof of the car. Lowering the trunk to look at the top of the car, I saw a raven flying away with my small bag of meat ends. I gave chase across the field, but the fucking black piece of shit pretended to stagger and then once I was out of breath it cruised to the top of a building and ate the meat right in front of me. Upon seeing this I burst into tears and stood there alongside the road crying and wailing at my misfortune and stupidity. Sniffling, I walked back to the car and ate two mustard sandwiches with tea. I knew then that was a low point and things would get better and, after a good sleep under the dance of the northern lights, they did.

I had found full-time work and was able to gain back some weight, but it seems the seeds of change of living in my car were already sown. One might think that if given a choice of winter

keremeye'us

or summer that the latter is the season to live in a Volvo, but you would be wrong. The problem is heat and bugs: the only relief from one is to invite the other. So as spring came and the cold days grew few it became more uncomfortable to remain a person of no fixed address.

The clincher was a day in late April. I was working as much as I could so my sleep was sporadic, but finally after several weeks of long days and nights, I was to get a Sunday off. After working the graveyard shift I drove back into town and thought that a deserted parking lot near the college would do. So, as I had not showered in two weeks and was grimy with dust and dirt, I decided to sleep nude. The sleeping bag I had was good for -30 C, so I unzipped it to allow some fresh, predawn air inside and then fell into a deep sleep.

Well, the daylight brought on some unusually warm temperatures and, all closed in within the car, the temperature rose to well over 30 C. I was so exhausted that I tore off the top of the bag in my sleep and was laying there at window height, completely naked. As fate would have it, the parking lot was an overflow for a large regional swim meet at the pool. It seems that, once discovered, I became a secret attraction for the kids, who gathered around and stared at me like a reptile in an aquarium.

Finally, some of the youth alerted the staff and then the peace officers were summoned, and I was essentially run out of town. Thankfully, there was no sicko watch list back then as I am sure I would have been placed on it. I decided then to rent a room in town and within a week I had to take my Volvo to an auto wrecker as it would not pass a safety inspection. I avoided the pool and got a haircut and over time no one connected the dots that I was the pervert sleeping in the car.

In the morning near the base of Turtle Mountain I rose before dawn. I was able to nurture the small fire back to life and watched the orange glow over the prairie below. It was the first time in the journey that I felt above the sunrise as its rays slipped down the mountains behind me. As the slopes yawned, a slow but continuous breeze flowed down the valley. As it warmed, the prairie tugged at the cool reservoirs trapped within

Joseph Woodcock

the great valleys to the west and, by the time I had packed up and began to walk, the wind pushed me eastward with the firmness of a giant hand. From that day and for another month the wind would be my greatest single source of adversity, and at times, as the snows had done in the mountains, would force me to seek shelter. The wind would not alter my route, but at times it would delay it.

By the time I passed through Lundbrek the wind was blowing over seventy kilometers an hour and while it was a significant benefit when at my back, it leaned on me like a drunk steer when at my sides. In the distance, broad lines of wind farms stretched over the ridges and their giant blades swept in planetary orbits around their centres. On the ridges, I wished for the shelter of the valley, but once in the dry creek beds, the wind howled as would a phantom and if not properly approached would rip the canvas from the frame of the rickshaw.

Once on the outskirts of Pincher Creek, I found that I had to make a two kilometer run into the town itself at a near perfect right angle to the wind direction. It was an incredible struggle and oftentimes one of the wheels of the rickshaw was off the ground even with my full weight trying to hold it firm. That night I rolled my rickshaw into a mini-storage unit and then, travelling north with a friend, took a few days off for a visit with my family.

When I returned a few days later, calmer conditions prevailed and I walked out of Pincher Creek travelling in a southeasterly direction. By mid-morning I had been invited for lunch by a Mennonite family and was picked up by car at the main road. They had prearranged with the farmer at the intersection to keep an eye on my equipment and we drove the few kilometers to their farm nestled in the rolling hills. It was a couple hours of wonderful food and great conversation.

I was asked what thoughts filled my mind during the long hours of travel. As I struggled to construct a few sentences that would encase all that I had experienced so far, one of the ladies said, "If it were me, I would use the time to really find God." That honest expression of her belief truly made me pause and in the afternoon as I walked along the back roads I looked inward and tried to define my feelings so far. Of course, everything was better—I felt better physically, slept better, food tasted so much better, and I loved the adventure, but her words unintentionally seemed to diminish my simple enjoyment.

It kept with me for the rest of the day and then into the evening and for the first time since the start of my journey, I lay awake, unable to sleep. Even though I felt the hand of God, I was only able to express the simple physical pleasures and perhaps something as shallow as the phrase, "It's great." Of course, I felt the spiritual—who could not have—but did the inability to verbalize or express my beliefs lessen the value or worth?

I had walked off of the main road some distance and pitched my tent atop a small rise. Somewhat distracted with the words she had spoken, I never noticed the incredible vantage point I had chosen to sleep. In the early morning hours, the sun seemed to touch just two places on earth, the top of my tent and the mountains just to the west of me. Still at their feet and under the brilliance of their glaciers, my small tent sat alone against the vast rolling hills of prairie.

While asleep the song of meadowlarks filled my dreams as the tent served as the highest point to attract a female. So it was that for hours each male would stand atop my tent and sing in search of his soulmate. So pure and honest was their plea that I could not interrupt and lay quiet and still, absorbing the intensity and truth in each and every note. I felt a great peace then, as if someone had whispered in my ear to simply "enjoy the ride."

I stepped out into the day and stretched with the warmth of the rising sun upon my back and the magnificent eastern slopes of the Rocky Mountains to my front. I thought of her words and convictions—they were so absolute. I should have been envious, as with her beliefs comes a community, but I have never felt alone. Simply, I was not searching for anything.

Joseph Woodcock

How could I? I was standing there, under the majesty of the mountains, as the meadowlarks' song danced across the grasslands. Envy was for now, a distant emotion.

keremeye'us

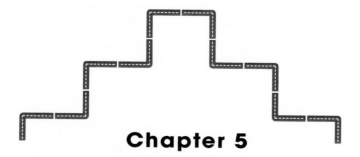

Chapter 5

At noon I pulled my rickshaw into the small hamlet of Glenwood. I was drawn in by the sign that the local restaurant was having its official grand opening, but it seems the sign went up a few days before the actual opening and I was left a bit disappointed. But within a few minutes I struck up a conversation with some locals and one of them drove home, made a pot of coffee, and brought it back. We all had a bit of a break there on the step of a business, and as a bonus a friend from years past who was working in the area stopped by. It was a fabulous time. Following the break I pulled out on the road and, after crossing the Belly River, entered the Blood Reservation lands.

That evening I took advantage of an area with no fences and pulled my rickshaw out into the prairie a bit, though still visible from the road. I was in the final stages of setting up my tent when I looked to the road, which was up above me and parked there was a Blood Tribe Police cruiser. Standing just upgrade from the cruiser was a large native police officer who was looking away from me, eastward, into the prairie. I knew this was Blood land and hoped there would not be a problem pitching a tent, but as I started to walk up the hill I wondered what he had in store for me.

As I walked the officer did not really look at me but was gazing all about suspiciously with a concerned look upon his face. As I climbed up the last few steps to the road he acknowledged me with a slight nod, but then turned again and continued looking all around. So, standing beside him, I did the same, and for what seemed like a minute we stood there staring out into the wide grasslands, not saying a word.

Then the large officer put his arm around me like a father might a son and gave me a bit of a shake. It was a friendly contact but still a bit odd, I thought. The officer sighed and then said, "Have you ever seen that movie about the wolf with Kevin Costner?" I was a bit taken back with the question, but happy the silence was broken and replied, "Yes. Dances with Wolves." Then I added, "Good message, good message," referring to the plight of the First Nations. He seemed pleased with my response as he pulled me in a bit closer and we stood again for another minute, nodding.

Speaking to me, but again looking to the rear, he asked, "Do you remember that scene where the young braves, all streaked with war paint and looking for trouble, stood on the hill and looked out over the vast prairie. They were pissed with the encroachment of the white man on their lands and were going to personally do something about it?" Remembering the scene well, I replied, "Sure, sure, they had bows and arrows and seemed cranky." "Right, right, yes, they were cranky and even the ponies looked a bit out of sorts," the officer said, now patting me on the back.

Again there was an extended period of nodding and then the officer continued to speak. "Do you remember that when those braves were standing there, looking out onto the vast prairie and appearing cranky, that they saw, far in the distance a small bit of smoke from a single camp fire?" "Yes, I remember that," I replied to the officer. The officer then pulled me close and said, "Just before the braves rode down to kill the white man and steal his mules, the one brave said to the others that only a white man would be so stupid as to build a fire on the prairie." "Right, yes, the smoke cold be seen for miles," I added as if I understood the message. "Well son, that bright orange tent of yours is like that campfire and if you wanted to tell all the cranky braves on this reservation that you are a white man on their lands, well you have certainly accomplished that."

Nervously chuckling I looked about as if an arrow was going to pierce my neck. The officer then took my cell phone and entered into speed dial every number he could think of me phoning, including the Chief's half-sister who lived just ten kilometers away, in case there was trouble. As he drove away I stared out at the seemingly empty prairie and then shuffled down to my tent. It was not the first time that felt a bit nervous, and like the last times I swore that I would sleep lightly. The problem is that I never sleep lightly and after a minute or two of listening to the coyotes howl, I closed my eyes and, it seemed, instantly awoke to the sound of the meadowlarks. Feeling a bit foolish at my nervousness and scoffing at the officer's concern, I packed up my gear and enjoyed the morning sun.

About a week later, though, I was entering the town of Milk River when a large car pulled up alongside me. In the car were several young native men. The driver nodded for me to come closer to the car window and when I did I saw he had two tattooed tear drops along his cheek—the tear drops signified that he had killed two men. They were a tough looking bunch, but the streets were busy and I was curious as to why they wanted to talk with me. After a few questions from them regarding the rickshaw and where I had walked and where I was going the driver asked if I was the one with the bright orange tent that had passed through the Blood lands. I replied that it was me and since the conversation seemed friendly and light, I told him about the funny story about the police officer. Of course he knew the officer and everyone in the car started to laugh.

Then the driver said, "We saw that bright orange tent and we had been drinking and wanted to come over, but we had watched that TV show Bait Car and we thought for sure the bright orange tent was a Bait Tent. We said that we were not going to fall for that stupid trap and instead went looking for some squaws." Everyone began to laugh. We shook hands and they offered me a warm beer, which I thought I should take, and then they rolled off out of town and into the prairie. Generally, after a conversation like that a person might think about carrying some personal protection, like in the form of a gun. It crossed my mind a few times, but I keep thinking back to when I was working in a logging camp in the Haida Gwaii, along the north coast of British Columbia.

I worked with a surveying and forest engineering group, so all of us liked the outdoors—especially fishing. In one corner of Masset Inlet was an abandoned logging camp that had once supplied Sitka spruce for the Mosquito Bombers of the Second World War. Of course, the camp had long been gone, but the old forest cover maps showed that a road once went from the camp, which was on the inlet, into the forest to a large lake. At the far end of the lake there were several creeks running into it, so we figured that the fishing would be fantastic.

Our plan was to have someone drop us off at the shore with two canoes and then we were going to hike up what was left of the road to the lake. Once on the lake we were going to canoe to the far end and camp on the beach. Initially it went well. The crew boat landed us on shore with the canoes and the five of us started into the timber. The first problem was the amount of gear we brought— by this I mean beer. The second critical problem was that there was no longer any road as the jungle had swallowed it up in the forty years since it was abandoned. Initially, we filled the canoes with our supplies and tried to carry them, but this proved ineffective. And it did not matter anyway, because the terrain was just too rough. By early in the afternoon we decided to abandon the canoes and carry in what we could to the outlet of the lake and make the best of it.

At the edge of the lake there was barely any shore, so we pitched camp along an extremely narrow strip of gravel. The forest and its underbrush hung over us. As we set up camp, one of the guys said he had forgotten his sleeping bag in the crew boat. By that time, though, we were all drinking scotch and smoking weed, so a missing sleeping bag did not seem relevant. It was still early March and at that latitude darkness comes early. After supper we sat at the campfire drinking and smoking. We had a fabulous meal of fish, so that was a positive, but it rained on and off and we were not well protected, so essentially, we were a bunch of stoned guys sitting in the rain.

It was a stormy night and the clouds raced by, exposing the moonlight across the dark water. That in itself would have been scary enough, but early on the guys started in on telling bear stories. By nine in the evening I was freaking out as each story was worse than the one before, but the weed and the liquor kept us going for another two hours or so. By the time we went to bed I was shaking with fear and to make things worse, just as I lay down, I saw these scratch marks into the fabric of the pup tent. I asked John what it was and he said a bear came by when he was hunting up north and scratched the tent before being run off. That was it. I almost started crying.

John and I were sleeping in his pup tent and the rest of the gang were in a poorly constructed lean-to. Both John and the others had rifles and I made sure that ours was loaded with a full clip and one shell in the barrel before going to sleep. It was only about midnight, but as John hit the sack he started to snore. I, on the other hand, stared into the darkness for a while before eventually succumbing to all the adventure of the day and also drifted away.

I was not sure of the time, but in the early morning hours I was startled awake by a noise. Immediately I thought of a bear nosing about in camp, perhaps drawn in by the fish we ate. I was frozen with fear, but my heart was racing as I could now clearly hear the bear grunting and pawing at the bones in the cold coals of the fire. I cannot explain the internal panic I was feeling, all I could think about was that rifle. In an attempt to save all of our lives I jiggled John violently, but as quietly as I could so as to not draw the beast in upon us.

John was not to be awakened easily, so I started punching and slapping him, all the time screaming silently in his face that we were under a bear attack. John, who was completely disorientated from the weed, beer, scotch, and mushrooms, started swatting me back as if I was attacking him. We were slapping each other and since he was making too much noise I was trying both to smother him and save his life. Finally he stopped struggling and I grabbed onto his ears and with my face in his screamed silently that a bear was going to kill us any second.

John rolled out his sleeping bag and looked at the tent door on his hands and knees. I will never forget the scene as John was just wearing a pair of old white underwear and I was nearly on his back. I had driven the loaded and now cocked rifle into his hands and pushed him forward to the door. Then the bear started making more noise and I lost all control. I was on John's back, holding his hair and screaming silently in his ears to shoot through the tent walls and kill the bear before he kills us.

John was waffling on my orders to pull the trigger so in the fight or flight survival response I lunged over him and tried to force the rifle away. It was a desperate struggle, both of us in our underwear rolling about the tent with a loaded and cocked rifle, all the time pointed at the tent entrance. He had his hand over the trigger and I was trying to pry off his fingers. I was sure he had gone mad. The bear was now sniffing at the door and I made one final, violent dive at the gun, but John rolled away and as the door opened I started to scream. It was then that Chester poked his head in and asked, "What the fuck is going on?" It seems that Chester, the one who had forgotten his sleeping bag, had awoken from the cold and was trying to get a fire going without disturbing the rest of the gang.

After spending a night in Cardston, I continued to head south until I reached the Alberta-Montana border. From here I turned east again and followed the road through Whisky Gap and then on to Del Bonita. These were some of the most scenic and inspiring days of my entire trek. The road generally runs on higher ground. To the west, the eastern slopes of the Rockies look forbidding and impassable and to the south, into Montana, the Sweet Grass Hills rise from the grasslands as if something from the African savannah.

Once into Del Bonita, I shared a coffee with two ladies at the only store there and then headed for the horizon on my way to Milk River. Traffic is rare along these roads and for a time both the grades and the winds were light. I always remember what my brother Mike said about the winds in southern Alberta. He spent a winter going to Lethbridge University, not far north of where I was, and told me about the wind. "In fact," he said, "one day the wind stopped, and everyone fell over." So I noted the soft breeze to my rear and was thankful, even if it was only for a day.

But the weather held and, after a quiet couple of days, I was nearing Milk River and thinking of getting a meal along with a room and a bath. My attention, though, was pulled away from those thoughts as I squinted to make out something against an old building. I could just see two rusty old handles and in walking closer, I found it was an old farming implement used for small lots, or in this case most likely a large garden. I am not sure if they ever had a proper name, but my father called ours "the Mule."

It was a large, heavy, single-cylinder motor, coupled to a transmission and gearbox, both of which had both power takeoff shafts to the rear and front. The entire unit was balanced on a single differential with two large and aggressive tires. From the rear extended two long handlebars with some linkage connected controls. If outfitted, the Mule could push snow, plow and rototill gardens, and, as I saw in China many years later, be equipped with a trailer in which the operator could stand. The Mule had very little ground speed but had the torque and gear reduction to move or pull almost anything, especially when fitted with tire chains. It had a single, two-stroke cylinder which rose and fell with long, lethargic momentum, as might a steam locomotive leaving a station. Beside all of the positive uses and attributes of the Mule, my father used ours to temporarily relieve our family from the scourge of mosquitoes.

keremeye'us

In Revelstoke in the dog days of summer, the heat and humidity was stifling. Trapped between the great mountain ranges, night felt like day, and with this and because of our location, surrounded by forest and moist skunk cabbage swamps, the bugs were insane. Not able to stay in the house due to the heat, and being eaten alive once outside, it was a constant struggle to find any relief. My father, though, a man of some ingenuity, came up with a solution. At mealtimes my mother would set everything up along two large picnic tables in the yard. My father would position the Mule just upwind, if there was any wind, and right beside the tables if there was not. He would only half fill the fuel tank with gas and then top off the other fifty percent with one part used motor oil and the other DDT. My mother loved a potent poison and with our connections to a brother-in-law in the farming business in Vernon, they were able to source high grade poisons easily.

The expulsion of the black smoke containing the lead-laced used motor oil probably would have been enough, but the DDT component killed even the bacteria and for the period during the meal and for a few hours afterward the area would be utterly void of any life other than the Woodcocks. The Mule barely ran as the mix was not that conducive to any sort of efficient operation and to restrain it even more, my father would peg the choke so its exhaust seemed to only puke out a massive cloud of smoke every few seconds. It was wonderful and all of us kids, after enjoying the meal, would run and play in the black smoke and lethal pesticide until the tank ran dry.

Those were happy times and I stood over the rusty old Mule at the roadside for a long period before rolling on down to Milk River and a tepid bath. In the morning, heading east of Milk River, one enters a small outback. The grass becomes sparse and the hills somewhat barren. It is an area of little rain and hot, arid winds. The creeks are dry and hoodoos and tiny cactus abound. Working family farms are few, replaced by large corporate or amalgamated co-operatives, and the crops, in the movement toward organically certified grains that require little attention, purge vast areas of equipment and people. There are farm houses and outbuildings, but they lean silent and dilapidated against the shiver of heat waves and the constant, moaning winds.

My plan at that point was to continue due east through this savannah and into the badlands of southern Saskatchewan. I was already questioning the reasoning of this route when I was visited one evening by a local rancher who had ridden his ATV for over an hour to find me. He examined my projected route on the maps and with a pencil and with great detail, drew in the only potable water sources for the next ten days; they were few. So I slept on this information as I still had a couple of opportunities to turn north and pick up roads with at least some services.

In the morning I awoke to light rains and a cold, northerly wind. It only took me a few steps to realize the trouble I was in as the clay road surface had turned to glue and within minutes the paste had formed large disks on the bottom of my shoes and the wheels skidded to a stop, each jammed solid. Throughout the morning I dragged the rickshaw through the gum, stopping every few minutes to scrape off the weight. By late morning I was exhausted and worse, the temperature had fallen and now wet snow blew against my left side providing constant frustration. A steep hill down into the dry bed of Lake Pakowki offered a temporary reprieve, but the climb out as the wheels brought up pounds of clay with each turn was grueling, and when I reached the top I just sank down onto my knees, soaking wet with sweat and gasping for oxygen.

I started looking for a place to camp, even though I had only been walking for a few hours. But just as I did a company pickup stopped and I was invited to have a coffee at a nearby gas compression plant. It was still a few kilometers along, but I found some new legs and just after noon, peeled off my muddy clothes and enjoyed a coffee and some lunch. It was a good break and gave me time to reflect on the vulnerable position I was in. The two people at the plant gave me a clear indication what the roads would be like in the days ahead given that the weather was to be wet and unsettled for the next week. That afternoon was a mirror image of the morning, with now heavy wet snows and increasingly poor conditions. The clouds had fallen right to the ground and visibility was poor. Any strength and motivation I had gained over lunch vanished and by midafternoon I was staggering along, again looking for a place to camp. But as in the morning, I was visited by a local man in a farm truck and he told me that just up the road were two outbuildings of a once-busy farming community. One was a church and the other a very small community hall. He said he was the caretaker, so to speak, of the grounds and I could stay in the coat room of the hall for as long as I wanted. I was so appreciative and thanked him so much but understood, from past experiences, that "just up the road" was still most likely hours away.

As the afternoon waned on, all became grey. The wind never let up and I forced myself into a continuous pace just to stay warm. There was no horizon and certainly no hint of any buildings, but I continued to trudge, stopping every few minutes to relieve the weight and burden of the mud. As darkness began to settle in, I lost all aspect of time and distance and ate whatever nutrition I could find at hand in the pack; pushing it down with litres of water. I never thought of stopping because I knew if I did, I would certainly find the hall early the next day and the thought of this drove me on, into the dusk.

Soon afterward I caught a glimpse of an outline and then again a few minutes later. Then the fractured pixels came together and through the snows, against a grey shadow, the definition grew into one, then two small buildings up to my left upon a long, gentle rise. As one final challenge, the road turned north at the base of the rise and for the final kilometer the snow and wind spat directly in my face as the road surface oozed and seeped. Every step had to be engineered and plotted, each time I slipped into an anxious and uneasy pose. Slowly, the splintered horizon crept downward and the two small structures grew until I turned into the driveway. Past the tiny church I walked to the hall and, opening my knife, slipped it into the lock as instructed. The wide door opened as the gasp of wind and snow blew into the darkness. I had made it. I forced a smile as two small mice ran along the base of the wall and darted into cover.

An hour later it was as if I was at home, the gas lantern illuminated the room and my pot of tea simmered in soft harmony to the storm outside the doors. I had changed into dry clothes and ate a couple of cans of stew and then something sweet the people at the gas plant had given me. I knew there was no opportunity to dry any of my clothes, but I had a good quantity and selection for several days. "Several days" though, stuck in my mind, and looking at the maps I projected the possible hardship that lay ahead of me if I continued due east. I had already today eaten two days' worth of food and my water consumption clearly outpaced my ability to replenish it at this pace. After a couple hours of pondering, I was both a bit disappointed and also excited to again feel a firm road surface under my feet.

In the little room attached to the small hall beside the church I enjoyed the physical shelter of the walls, but also, again, the shelter of kindness. Once again I had been the recipient of shelter with nothing asked in exchange. In the middle of a sweeping and vast landscape, pressed tight between the colourless earth and sky, I slept as a child as the mice rummaged through my gear. The next day, in the early afternoon, I stepped off of the muddy surface and onto a paved road leading north and let out a pleasant sigh. Though the sleet and wind continued, I relished each long stride and by nightfall, enjoyed a warm meal and a soft bed in the small community of Manyberries.

I spent one night in Manyberries and the next day headed north. I had wanted to travel through the Cypress Hills, but I talked with some locals who said that snows still covered most of the park's roads and learned that the forecast for cool, changeable weather was to continue for some time. It was good advice and a good decision to follow it because the next few days were cold and incredibly windy. I set a slow pace north

keremeye'us

and arrived in Medicine Hat with the intent of spending a few days at rest. Again a smart decision because on the second day I came down with the flu. So my few days became five, but it was a good forced break, one which I mostly slept in the tub.

When I did leave Medicine Hat the consensus was that this spring would continue to be cooler and windier than normal. So with this in mind and few options immediately available, I decided to stay on the TransCanada Highway until at least Swift Current and weigh my options there. Again, this proved to be a positive move as the days were a mix of snow and rain until I pulled into a rest stop at Maple Creek. It was only noon, but as I got myself together to get a coffee at the restaurant, the westerly wind came to an abrupt stop. I don't think there was more than a minute of calm when the wind changed direction and started to blow from the east at sixty kilometers an hour. By the time I had finished my lunch, it was a blizzard and there was already talk of the highway being closed due to poor visibility. I immediately booked a room for the night in the small motel at the back of the lot.

The motel and gas station were operated by at least two Korean families. The motel had been built many years before and, I think, was designed as something with a "theme", possibly an attraction or at least an oddity that may bring visitors back. The motel was built with none of the walls or ceilings or anything else at right angles, so everything except the floor was at an angle or sloped in some way. One could easily get disoriented—I found it difficult to sit on the toilet seat without hanging onto the wall as it seemed I was going to slide off.

When walking down the hall, even some of the windows leaned out and gave me a bit of a feeling of vertigo—at times I felt almost nauseous. The first day it was a bit of a nuisance, but as the storm lingered into day two and three, it began to wear on me. There was little to distract one from the dizzy sensation as the TV did not work and if one was able to secure a wireless connection it was short-lived as any truck that circled the motel to access the diesel pumps drove between the rooms

Joseph Woodcock

and the transmitter, thus cutting the signal. I felt I was slowly going mad, so I tried to spend my waking hours in the near-deserted restaurant.

The restaurant was operated by a young Korean man, perhaps nineteen years of age. His modified sports car sat in one of the stalls under two feet of snow. He said his father bought the gas station and restaurant as a family business, but the rest of the family, including his father were nowhere to be found. The young man said that before he moved there a few months earlier, he had only been in two places in his whole life. One was North Vancouver, and the other was Seoul, South Korea. He was clearly having a difficult time adjusting to his new life as he just stood, blindly looking out of the restaurant windows at the bald-ass prairie. Continuously mumbling and shaking his head, it was impossible to get any service, and some customers came in hungry and went out hungry, slamming the door as they left.

We kept each other company during the long blizzard, but as faithful and as dutiful as an Asian son can be, he said if he could just get his doors unfrozen and the car to start, he would just run away. I felt sorry for him and tried to cheer him up by saying that perhaps in a few years his family will send out a bride for him. My joke did not go well as he cupped his hands over his face. I immediately apologized for my insensitivity and blamed it on "those fucking walls, all this way and that—It's driving me fucking nuts."

Camping alongside the frozen Christina Lake, BC

Joseph Woodcock

The summit of Bonanza Pass, BC

Crow's Nest Highway near Fernie, BC

Joseph Woodcock

Crow's Nest Summit, BC-Alberta border

Looking back at Rockies, SW Alberta

Joseph Woodcock

Rouleau(Dog River), Sk

keremeye'us

Hard day's end. Southern Manitoba

Joseph Woodcock

Bemidji, Minn, USA

keremeye'us

Crossing the Mississippi River, Minn, USA

Joseph Woodcock

Dean lake Bridge, Ont.

Quebec City

Joseph Woodcock

Western shore of Newfoundland

keremeye'us

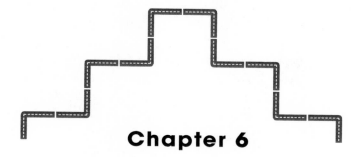

Chapter 6

When the weather improved slightly I headed east again. With little definition to the landscape and gloomy conditions, I stretched out my stride and each day would travel between forty and fifty kilometers. With the availability of gas stations and restaurants to rest up, I concentrated on reaching Swift Current. Though I had many people stop and chat, traffic on the TransCanada Highway was all going somewhere quickly, so the long days were filled with reflection. One soggy morning, in the drone of passing traffic, a rusty old Chevrolet Malibu shuffled by me, its fenders and quarter panels completely rusted out. I started to laugh.

In the mid 1990s, Kitten, myself, our two young children, and Muffy the dog were living in northern Ontario. We had moved there for good work with benefits and relative security. But, of course, I quit that and went into a risky venture with an Ojibwa fellow operating a small sawmill on band lands. It was not long before this enterprise went bust and we found ourselves broke and far from our home province of British Columbia. The need to get the family back west felt pressing. I borrowed a few hundred dollars from my brother and, with half of that stuffed in my pocket, went looking for a car.

Well, I ran into the right salesman—he drove me out into the countryside and beside his recently deceased mother's barn was a 1982 Malibu. The grass and weeds were growing right up through the floorboards and the paint was peeled and chaffed. The wheel wells were almost double their original diameter with rust and decay. Opening the hood, I heard the scurry of rodents and found the unit had no battery, no coolant, no air filter, and just a slight taste of black engine oil. All four tires were flat and if you could get the trunk open, you could look down and see the ground. The windshield was fractured and the sun had peeled up the dashboard in great heaves. Any suspension had collapsed and the odour of mold and rotting upholstery brought on the gag reflex. On the negative side, it was registered in Ontario and because of the year, it would have to be inspected before one could license it.

The dealer, who sold cars in an abandoned lot across from the smelter, said he could work the papers somehow that I could drive it to British Columbia and get it licensed there. So after agreeing on a price of $350, which included an old battery, I spent a couple of hours inflating the tires and, with a boost from his Lincoln, the Malibu burst back to life. He was concerned that if it was to start, it may catch the grass on fire, so as soon as it started to rumble I jammed it into gear, tore around in a tight shit-hook and thundered across the yard and up onto the road. There were mice and shrews bailing out from all sides, the trunk flew up and bounced along like a massive Beaver's tail, one headlight fell out, and the front bench seat flipped backward as it tore from the rusted anchors.

I realised I had no brakes as the fluid had seeped out of the corroded lines but I found that in neutral the car came to a rapid stop, though it continued to rock and sway for some time afterward. I threw my weight against the door, the hinges moaned, but, inch- by-inch, I jostled the door open. The tires were skins and the exhaust system, which I reinforced with coat hangers and asbestos tape, sort of floated and flexed with the motion of the ride. I found the gas tank had a leak in the top third of it, but it was easy to plug as I had unobstructed access from the trunk, and, basically, there were few working electrical components. But given the price, if pointed in a straight line, the "Chick Magnet" as we called it, would dance behind the 350 V8's muscle.

I found work in Fort Nelson, British Columbia and Muffy and I drove the Chick Magnet out from Ontario. Kitten was to hold "the man" at bay until she could perform a midnight move a month later. On emergency welfare, her car repossessed and belongings sold in the driveway, she rustled the kids together in the middle of the night and took the bus to Toronto. Not able to afford headphones, the kids ate food bank rations and watched several Kung-Fu movies in silence during the pre-dawn exodus.

Once somewhat settled in Fort Nelson, and in the midst of winter with no working heater fan in the car, the family needed some downtime. To celebrate our good fortune, we packed up for a weekend in Fort St. John, which was just like Fort Nelson, but because it was four hours to the south, it boasted a milder average winter temperatures by at least three degrees. The Chick Magnet seemed to perform better in -38 C conditions, perhaps because it was frozen together, so it was not long before we were up to speed, dodging caribou and playing Xs and Os with the scraper on the inside of the windshield. The kids, who hugged Muffy for warmth, dined on hot chocolate and frozen peanut butter and jam sandwiches also enjoyed the loud games designed to keep them awake as Kitten feared they may slip into a never-ending sleep.

As we sailed blindly along I caught sight of an exceptionally large pothole in the middle of the highway. The Chick Magnet was originally built with no manoeuvrability and at this stage in its life it consisted of two separate entities, one the rusty body, and the other everything else. Holding the two together was for the most part just gravity, so any attempt to steer around the large hole was futile. Bracing ourselves, we hit it hard. There was a terrific crash and car body parts, including the passenger mirror, plates of rusty metal, and half of the rear bumper, littered the highway. The trunk flew open and the interior of the roof collapsed onto Kitten who was screaming and flailing about. The radio, which had never worked, started to crackle and, somehow, Muffy ended up on my lap. It took us a couple of seconds to take inventory but quickly felt relief that everyone was unhurt and the sled was still on the road. I was trying to pry pooch from my lap when Jessica said she could see the road. This was odd because she was sitting low in the back seat and besides that, the windshield resembled those glass blocks you see in public buildings.

Upon inspection Kitten began to scream again as sections of the floor in the back seat had fallen out. The highway and a swaying section of the exhaust system, wrapped in grey asbestos tape were within touch. Kitten, whom I sometimes think looked at the negative too much, began to freak out with possible accounts of the kids being dragged under the car. Once calmed down with a couple of Valium in her, Kitten took the wheel and with both kids and Muffy in the front seat, I sat in the rear for the remainder of the drive.

A few months later, in late spring, I was fired from that job and was several weeks into my job search on southern Vancouver Island. I spent my days floating down the Cowichan River on inner tubes as Kitten continued to attempt to give the kids some semblance of normalcy far to the north. Through involvement with a local swim club Kitten, Muffy, and the kids were travelling in the Chick Magnet to Dawson Creek for a swim meet. The hot temperatures, combined with heavy thunderstorms, pushed up the humidity to unbearable levels. As they left Fort Nelson torrential rains followed them south and, without warning, the windshield wipers stopped working.

Kitten, determined, drove the last three hours with her head out the side window and along the way picked up quite an assortment of bugs and insects, all tangled up and struggling for release from within her dark waves. Arriving a bit late for the meet Kitten, who always liked to look her best, was soaked from the waist up and her hair was strung out behind her like a sculpted cape. As she did her best to get a brush through it a cricket struggled to get free. Kitten tried to ignore the stares and apologized profusely as coaches and other mothers jumped back in shock and yelled, "Holy Jesus!"

Joseph Woodcock

A short time later we moved into a small townhouse in the Cowichan Valley; I had found some work and we enjoyed the benefits of family and friends close by. Still somewhat financially strapped, but on the mend, I rode my bike the fifteen kilometers each way to work and Kitten and the family relied on the Magnet to shuttle them around. As things improved a bit financially, Kitten was on the hunt for a better ride and had her eyes on a new minivan. Throughout the wet winter, it was a constant discussion; me pointing out that the sled still ran and was costing us nothing and Kitten pointing out that "It's a piece of shit."

In fairness, we started to have some problems with it regarding reliability and even the kids, noting their friends' parents would not let them ride in it, began to turn against it. Muffy, though, well, I think we were tight. However, one week later things started to unravel as occasionally the Magnet would not start and Kitten and the kids would find themselves walking home in the rain. I put off the repairs until the weekend and as it approached I was feeling the pressure as there was some sort of attraction or occasion where Kitten and the kids wanted to be and I was given several ultimatums.

I did not know it then, but the root of the Chick Magnet's final run had begun nearly a year earlier. When I started my new job in a wood processing facility in Chemainus, one of my duties was to get the equipment operating before the crew arrived. In the torrential rain, I pushed the button for the garage door but nothing happened. Again a few times but nothing. Right about then our maintenance man came along and I showed him. He scratched his chin for a few seconds and then walked to his shop and came back with a delicate, small cardboard box.

He opened the box and lifted off a styrofoam cover. Inside was a small, lipstick-sized aerosol container. Shutting off the power to the disconnect and then removing the cover of the control button for the door, he took the small spray bottle and gave a gentle squirt of liquid to the contacts. He then allowed a full five minutes for the aerosol to dissipate before placing the covers back on. When he did push the button, the door lumbered up and down. I was so

keremeye'us

impressed that I wanted to buy some, but he said that this was just coming on the market and was not approved and that he got it through someone who knew someone else. But the demonstration stayed with me.

Months later as Kitten and the kids gave me the stink eye regarding the Magnet, I thought of that electrical contact spray. Opting to not buy a starter, I decided to pocket the savings and rebuild the old one. So at the automotive parts store early that Saturday morning, already feeling the panic and pressure of getting the sled running by 10:30 so Kitten and the kids could attend the festival, I bought some new components and, almost as if guided by angels, saw there on the end of the row large aerosol cans of this electrical contact fluid. It was clearly a win in my column and I purchased one of the large cans, which contained a 33% volume bonus, and bounded out of the store. I was so excited, as it was exactly the same product as we had used on the garage door the year before, only five hundred times more so.

After arriving home I quickly crawled under the car and removed the starter motor. We were not allowed to do any mechanical work on vehicles in the complex, so I edged around to our back step and began to disassemble the motor. It came apart easily and I spread the components of the cylinder along the walkway, all the while hearing negative comments from the kids, who had now clearly turned against me. Even Muffy took on a disapproving and impatient stance, apparently somewhat irritated that he may miss a few minutes of the parade.

With the trash talk and innuendos echoing out of the screen door, I felt the pressure build; I scraped and cleaned the components as fast as I could. The entire time, which was only a few minutes, I doused the interior electrical components with the cleaning fluid. Then, sliding each piece back into the metal cylinder one at a time, I used the spray almost continually until I came to the cover. Starters are like a genie—once the electrical winding and guts are out of the shell they want to fly everywhere, so I was concentrating on holding it all together. Just before I placed the cap back on I emptied the final contents of the contact fluid into the gap and then sealed it up.

I was excited and clearly cocky as I rolled back under to the car to reinstall the motor. I had yelled in through the open window that the unit will be ready in five minutes and took some personal pleasure in hearing my family start to natter at each other—they had little faith in me, and now, with the Chick Magnet almost ready to roll, each of them felt that they were in the sights. As I fumbled to reattach the starter motor back onto the flywheel, the kids and Muffy bailed into the front seat with Kitten, wearing an attractive blue sundress, in behind the wheel. I was not going to the festival, but if I were, I would have been sitting in the back seat as always because everyone else, including Muffy, refused to, citing the missing floor as a reason. Regardless of the non-invite, I relished in my triumph and rolled out of the grass and invited Kitten to fire her up.

There was a second or two pause—I have the picture of all of them there in the Chick Magnet engrained in my memory. Kitten found her keys and just before sliding on her sunglasses gave me a playful little glance. I found her tantalizing and erotic in her sundress, her thick, dark hair shimmering against the sun. Then, for a second, Kitten flashed me a bright, wide smile of affection. The kids and Muffy all turned toward me in unison and, through the shattered windshield, seemingly validated not only my regard and confidence in the sled, but my overall minimalist and pious beliefs: this was true wealth.

Of course, I did not try to make a bomb, but as Kitten turned the key and the surge of electrical energy burst into the copper windings flooded with high-grade accelerant and confined within a metal cylinder, that is exactly what it was. The explosion launched the front end of the Chick Magnet right off of the ground and the deafening boom and shock wave knocked me back against the stucco wall of the complex. The blast shattered the section of the flywheel securing the starter motor, which, after striking the car firewall and oil pan, skittered across the parking lot like a cruise missile. The other tenants of the complex, who were mostly were recent immigrants from war-torn countries, dove to the ground

keremeye'us

and shrieked out warnings in assorted languages that there was "incoming." The hysterical screams of an elderly woman from an open window echoed between the row houses as the rumble of the detonation rolled out across the neighbourhood.

As the Chick Magnet's front wheels hit the pavement, Kitten's glasses flew off and the car filled with smoke. The interior ceiling again fell down and the kids struggled and fought under its weight. Everyone was screaming and Muffy was barking as Kitten scrambled to evacuate everyone from the car. Once safe, they all stormed into the apartment and slammed the door. A Somali neighbour dragged back the casing of the starter motor by its cable and threw it in my yard and on Monday evening, after a quiet Sunday, I rode my bike home from work and found, in place of the Chick Magnet, a new minivan.

I spent a couple nights in Swift Current and, with the weather still cool, I continued to walk due east along the TransCanada. This was another period of long physical days, but with anywhere and everywhere to pitch a tent and always a truck stop to look forward to, I simply enjoyed the rhythm. What I did not realize at the time was that my regular pace and long days were doing me harm. I first noticed the change in my step, as it seemed my toes slapped against the pavement like a cartoon duck. I tried to avoid this, but unless I controlled every step, I found that it returned. At first it was an oddity and then a couple of days later my entire stance seemed contorted as if it was trying to overcorrect.

The problem was two things: The first was that, due to the flat prairie, my walking position never changed—I never pulled uphill to any degree or stretched out-- all of the impact was isolated to just one area of my legs. The second was the long days—twelve to fourteen hours of almost continuous speed walking. One morning, just to the west of Moose Jaw, in the middle of a field, I slipped out of my cot and fell onto the floor of the tent. It was as If my shins had been chopped by an axe and, unless I measured every simple step, I could not walk. I was sure it was shin splints and was angry with myself for not

Joseph Woodcock

taking more care and attention. That day I spent resting in the tent, but with only one day's distance from Moose Jaw I thought it best to try and get there. Once in Moose Jaw I could perhaps rent a room for a week and rest. The worst of it was that it was extremely painful.

In the first few weeks of caring for my father, it became clear that he was addicted to several things, and one of them was medication. He took quite a cocktail of heavy painkillers; the most prevalent were Oxycontin and Percocet. Over time his consumption of these, along with other narcotics and alcohol, fell to almost nothing and it was not long before I found I had a drawer full of pills. Almost all went back to the drug store, but I kept about ten of each just in case.

As I lay there in the tent on the side of the highway I peered through the old pill bottle containing the medication. I needed to get to Moose Jaw. Very early in the morning, I swallowed some of each and started to limp down the highway. Though the next hours are a bit hazy, I remember stopping several times to ingest some more, but that is about all I remember. In the early afternoon a courteous front desk clerk escorted me, the rickshaw still strapped to my back, through the Motor Inn parking lot to a nice room with a soft bed—it was a "man down" situation.

I spent two days just shifting from the bed to the bath, applying hot then cold compresses to my shins, and reading. Sorting through my equipment I found the pill bottle and rolled it in my hand. I read the label and my father's name and I felt a bit of a chill. That afternoon my family contacted me to inform me that my father had passed away—my sister Cathy had watched his spirit rise from him as she sat by his side.

Upon returning to Regina from the service, I took a bus to Moose Jaw and rolled my rickshaw out of the storage unit. Leaving the TransCanada, I headed southeast in a straight line toward Weyburn. It was now certainly summer and a warm steady breeze swayed the pastures in waves. For the next month the travelling would be simple and enjoyable—the warm, dry conditions and small farming communities allowed a balanced mix of solitude and conversation. As I paralleled the railway tracks the crews waved and honked at me each day. Traffic was light and people were friendly and each day melted into the next. I continued to be cautious about my distance and looked for any signs of fatigue, but there were none. With each town having at least one grain elevator, I could usually see my day's destination by first coffee. Reading good books and watching prairie storms passed the nights, and, of course, my father was on my mind throughout.

I picked up a new pair of walking shoes that my daughter had mailed me at the post office in Carlyle, and the day after that I was chased into Redvers by thunder and heavy rain. I had been fortunate over those past two weeks regarding weather so took the forecast for a couple days of rain in stride. I booked a room at a local motel, enjoyed a bath and walked to the diner for a meal. Once there, I met some people and was invited to spend the next day with them. After being picked up in the morning, we went for breakfast and then, after a tour of the countryside, had an enjoyable lunch at his daughter's. After a day of great conversation, I caught up on my laundry and relaxed.

The next day I crossed into Manitoba, welcomed by lush fields and clear skies. I again fell into a nice pace and I savoured the simplicity of each day. One evening, just after setting up camp, a small pickup pulled up and the male driver, along with a beautiful native woman, delivered me some wild rice soup and bannock she had made just that day. Neither of them was much for conversation and as quickly as they came they were gone. The food was excellent and the woman reminded me of another young woman I had met years before on the side of the highway.

I was working and living in northern Alberta, but my children were still on Vancouver Island. Kitten and I were separated. I was planning a trip down to visit them and was fussing about trying to get things in order when I received a phone call from Kitten saying that the kids were going camping that weekend, so there was no

Joseph Woodcock

rush to get there before that. This was good, so I took my time and left for the coast on a Thursday summer morning.

I was driving an old car that basically was the Dodge version of the Chick Magnet. I had been under a bit of passive pressure from my employer to buy something of better quality. The car had spawned some rumours that my poor personal finances were a direct result of addiction and lifestyle issues. After some prodding from his peers, my boss had taken me aside and after some fumbling with how to broach the subject of drug addiction, pointed to the car and stated, "You must have a wicked crack habit."

As I drove west along the Yellowhead Highway I noticed a small car on the side of the road with the hood up. Nudging off of the pavement I backed up and stepped out. The car was a tiny Chevette Scooter and standing beside it was a very attractive girl with long black hair. Though she was visibly upset, she was trying to mask it. I asked her a couple of questions, but she could only come up with the car had stopped several times that day. It was a simple engine and could only be a few things, so I started to eliminate the obvious ones.

The girl was not too forthcoming with details and a couple of times she snapped at my questions, but in seeing her distress, I tried to remain level-headed. I got her car started and I convinced her to switch vehicles with me until we reached the town of Hinton, or until her car stopped again, whichever came first. She agreed and I drove off in her Chevette with her in my car. It was not long, though before the small car sputtered and I had to pull over. I told her it was most likely a fuel problem, but since she was already on empty, I said we should get some fuel and a couple other things from a hardware store in Hinton, just a few miles away.

I told her that she could wait there, or she could come with me and if she was hungry we could get a burger or something. Well you can understand her quandary, either sit on the side of the highway or get into an old wreck with a longhaired stranger. I expected her to choose the first option, but, after some time, she opted for the second. I made some room for her and tried to keep the conversation light on the way into town. I knew she was nervous so I told

keremeye'us

her in advance a few times that the large hardware store was on the far side of Hinton.

Unfortunately, she didn't understand my meaning and was starting to freak out a bit as we drove right through Hinton and looked as if the next stop was the mountains. Unbeknownst to me, she had been searching for the door handle, which on the passenger side had broken off months earlier, making her escape seemingly impossible. Even though her licence plates were from Ontario, it would be hard for her not to know of the steady coverage in every newspaper regarding all of the women who had gone missing on that road, a stretch that had been coined "the highway of death."

Just before the large sign appeared for the hardware store, she began to come totally unglued and was trying to roll down the window to scream for help. She was in such a state though, she was trying to roll the handle the wrong way and let out a bark when I leaned over to help her. By the time we rolled into the parking lot she was in full terror mode and I wanted to get out as much as she did. Screeching to a stop I jumped out and ran around to open her door. Not only did she leap out but ran some distance away swatting at the air as if I was trying to pull her down. I was still standing at the car, kind of hoping she would just keep running. I ignored her and went into the store and picked up a gas can and some things I thought I might need. I still was not sensitive to her fears because when I came back out she asked me what I bought and out of the four items, three—a rubber hose, tape, and a knife were well known "rape kit" items. I mean, even I was beginning to question my intentions.

I got her some water and she ate a piece of goat cheese and something green from her packsack and started to calm down a bit. I, on the other hand, was just starting to realise the situation I was in. Once back at the Scooter I put some gas into it and drained a fuel filter. Sputtering away it made it into Hinton and we pulled over at a wide spot in the road. So I told her that I was not sure if it was the gas I put in or the filter or both or neither but that I was in no hurry and, like herself, was driving to Vancouver. I said that we could travel together or if she preferred I could give her some *money to get the car repaired by a garage. I told her that I had some money and it was no problem, but she very quickly rejected the idea of the garage and like most of the conversations, she was short on details as to why. So there we stood for some time in silence as she pondered the options. It was clear that she was short on money for some reason, so I broke the silence and said that I could help her out some with gas and such. At this point she agreed that we could travel together.*

So, with daylight fading, I suggested that we go to the gas pumps and fill both cars. Once at the pumps she began to fill her little car and I, right across the gas island from her, was filling mine. I think she was having second thoughts at the sight of the mountains ahead, or perhaps she could read the headlines on the newspapers regarding all the disappearances or who the hell knows, but she began to act agitated and was staring at me suspiciously. In return, I was thinking, "What kind of stupid chick would head into the mountains with a longhaired, middle-aged man driving an old rusty piece of shit?"

So there we were, our minds racing but neither of us actually talking. Finally, looking at the time and to break the silence I jokingly asked her, "You must be tired of Hinton?" referring to the hours we have spent in the area. She cocked her head and glared right at me. A bit confused and thinking perhaps she did not hear me, I leaned over to her and said again, "You must be tired of Hinton?" and added a little wink and a smile. She dropped the gas nozzle on the pavement and stepped back, looking startled.

It was a late Thursday afternoon on a long weekend and the gas station was packed with travellers trying to fill up before heading into the mountains. The convenience store lineup for the till stretched out the door and it seemed everyone either was reading about all these missing women or talking about it. So it was then, in the midst of this paranoia that the beautiful, dark-haired girl started screaming at me that she was "not hinting at anything" and that "you are some sort of perverted killer-freak," and on it went. I was thinking it could not get worse when a group of what looked like Australian rugby players descended into the

keremeye'us

situation. She was wigging out and going on about her "not hinting at anything" and he had a rape kit and her car had broken down and on it went. I was thinking about just running away, but felt sure it was what the team was looking for, so I stood my ground and just kept pointing at the "Welcome to Hinton" sign and noting that we had been there all afternoon.

Finally, it started to sink in to her that I was not saying "hinting" but was, in fact, saying "Hinton." I think the boys were looking for a rope to drag me behind the bus when it finally hit her and she buckled over in shock. Now trying to disarm the bomb, both she and I tried to talk down the mob who clearly had some inertia. Someone mentioned the police and I piped in that I was in agreement with that. "Yes, please, call the cops," I said, fearing now a vigilante situation was close at hand. I mean, I hardly believed myself and look at the car: the trunk could have easily been full of torsos. She was even less convincing—amid nervous laughs she tried to lend some levity to the situation by spouting off about "no passenger door handle and a trick window...to trap his prey."

Finally, it was the low price of gas that broke the deadlock. A couple of the motorhomes decided that the price at the pump was too good to miss and started honking. This forced some movement and with this I ran in and paid for both pumps and, soaking wet with sweat, begged her to stop talking and to follow me out onto the highway. Once up to speed I found I could not stop shaking and welcomed the rush of air through the side window.

Her little car died once more at Jasper, but after the elimination of the other possibilities in Hinton, I found it was a corroded electrical connection at the fuel pump and had it repaired in just a few minutes. Although I knew that it made no jurisdictional difference, I still felt relief when we passed over the British Columbia-Alberta border and I welcomed the darkness of the evening. We pulled into Little Fork a few hours later I got her a room. Then I collapsed in the back seat of my car.

The next morning we drove to Kamloops and sat down at a restaurant. It was then that she became quite chatty and told me that she had left Ontario a week earlier, but her car had broken

Joseph Woodcock

down several times. Each time she had to get a tow to a mechanic who started it up and took her money, only for it to soon breakdown again. With this she spent most of her money and when it broke down again in near Hinton, she was desperate. During the conversation she mentioned her family back home and that she had not spoken with them since she left for university a week earlier.

I quickly put things together that, in her parents' eyes, she was considered missing. This was before cell phones, so I gave her my credit card and made her go right out to the pay phone to contact her parents. It seems the timing was right because her mother, at her wits end, had invited over all of the church members and they were in the middle of a vigil, praying if not for her safe return, then at least a body. The phone rang, her mother answered and everyone began to cry and thank the Lord. That evening we parted ways on the outskirts of Vancouver, she going onto graduate studies and I carried on to visit my children.

keremeye'us

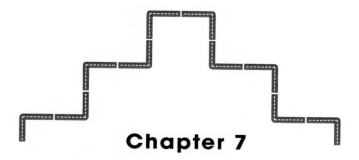

Chapter 7

Walking through the towns of Souris and Wawanesa in south-ern Manitoba one gets a feeling that they are in the deep south-eastern US. The Souris River winds like a serpent through idyllic pastures, its banks draped with foliage. Swallows slip into the clay cliffs or dangle from abandoned trestles, and once it becomes dark bats flutter and swoop between creosote pilings, silhouetted against the moon; across the silent, lazy waters one hears the "tick" of June bugs as they fall prey. The soft wake of a muskie creeps across the channel, and as though almost an illusion, the lethargic, smoky waters contort to the displace-ment below and then settle, soft again, to display the distorted echoes of the heavens above. The chorus of the night flexes and falls, and slowly starts up again. It rises and rolls, like the ebb and flow of the tide, across the meadows. Each night I closed my eyes to this ovation, this soft applause, and attempted to count my blessings. It was futile though, as sleep came almost immediately. My whispers eroded to thoughts and then to dreams as, softly, my lips continued to form each appreciative word in silence.

I detoured north and, literally running from the storms, I

dodged under canopies and shelters until I entered the small hamlet of Elie, not far from Winnipeg. I had friends there and enjoyed the comforts of pleasant company and terrific food before receiving news that my Aunt Vickie had passed away in Revelstoke, British Columbia. I rolled my rickshaw to the rear of their garage and flew back west once again to the place of my birth. Vickie was the last of my mother's siblings. After the war she had taken the train across the continent from New York into the majesty of the Rocky Mountains. First visiting, then settling, she met her husband-to-be at a local dance and then spent the rest of her life within the embrace of the splendour, enjoying days of broad smiles and laughter. My memories of her include her singing in the kitchen, preparing tea and honey sandwiches for me and my cousin, and her periods of silence to savour in appreciation of the peace.

I skirted around Winnipeg and wandered south, against the northward flow of the Red River. Each community along the way presented its historical conflict with the spring river floods. Photos, some newly stained with watermarks, decorated the tiny enclaves as testament to the stubbornness of the inhabitants. Earth and crumble dikes encircled like ancient walls, the gravity and weight of the river lumbering past them— patiently watching and waiting. This area seemed to have a history of both strife and fortune; the communities and colonies have defined boundaries, like fortresses. It gave me an isolated feeling as I worked my way south toward the border.

My view of the corridor was temporarily dimmed a bit more when the RCMP stopped me on the side of the highway. The officer said that there had been many complaints phoned in regarding my walking on the road. I asked who would complain about someone walking and he said that the highway is a busy truck route and the calls were from drivers. A little cranky about the situation, I tapped several discarded soft drink containers filled with urine and another couple of empty energy drink cans with my foot. Then I sarcastically asked, "The same drivers who can't pull over to sleep and then toss their piss out the windows?" He smiled and coolly replied, "Yes, probably the same ones."

He then said if I wanted to continue to walk on that road I would need a parade permit or if I preferred I was allowed to walk on the left hand side of the road facing traffic, but neither I nor my rickshaw could be on the paved surface at all. I looked at my map and saw that I would be able to exit the highway to an alternate route by the end of that day. He said that would be acceptable, but stated, "Starting right now, and until you reach that exit, you must keep well off of the paved surface."

So, sort of regretting my sarcastic remarks regarding the urine, I trudged along in the ditch for six full hours before pulling the burden back up onto the pavement at the exit. Even though I was exhausted from the portage, I think it was what I needed to clear my head. He was a likeable person and just doing his job, and before we parted he reached out to shake my hand. That was something at least. Also, when he checked up on me in the mid-afternoon he gave me a wave in appreciation, so, all in all, I thought he was all right.

The incident also opened my eyes to the better and safer option of walking on the left, facing the traffic. Across half of the continent, I relied on my mirrors, my eyes always darting back and forth like some kind of ferret or something. Now the possible danger was right in front of me and that bit of eye contact with the driver seemed to bring out a few more waves and smiles. The next year, while walking in Ontario, this improved vantage allowed me to swing the canopy out of the way of a full litre of piss being hurled my way from an irritable trucker, and one cannot put a price on that. By the time I walked into the border town of Emerson, I was back to my jovial self.

I got a motel room in Emerson as I wanted to go through my equipment carefully before trying to cross into the US the next morning. Among the items I thought would not be accepted was my collection of dead bird parts. In the months of walking, I had picked up and dried a few dozen wings and claws, beaks, bills, and skulls from dead raptors. These I gave

keremeye'us

to a few local kids the next day who were going to use them to freak out their sisters.

I had also been given a bottle of homemade wine from an elder in one of the Hutterite colonies I visited. Hutterites are generally heavily discouraged from drinking alcohol, but for some reason this colony had quite a wine cellar. Since I don't drink, I gave the bottle of wine to the motel owner, who, I am sure, gave it to someone else after I told him where I got it. The next item was a small block of homemade laundry soap that another colony gave me. It was wrapped in cellophane and genuinely looked like a brick of partially manufactured cocaine, so I used it up that evening and gave my gaunchies a wash.

With everything in place on the rickshaw, I got cleaned up myself and organised my passport and such. I enjoyed a pleasant evening on the porch and I began to think about the week past and why I had felt a bit melancholy. I was sure that the death of my father and my Aunt Vickie in such a short span played a part. Looking back, I could see that I had been avoiding close contact with people and had certainly felt the results of that. In looking at the map of the northeastern US, I felt I would have to put myself "out there" more and make the sometimes-difficult step of asking for assistance or advice. I did not know it then, but this simple task was to enhance my overall trekking experience.

Waiting in line at the border with traffic was priceless. As I stood there between two trucks, one and then all of the remote cameras turned to point at me. The guard at the booth waved me up and without any emotion asked me for my paperwork, like I was the tenth rickshaw that morning. Once he saw I had proper paperwork and there was no obvious reason for turning me back, he seemed to have a bit of a vested interest in getting me through. His phone rang, he answered with a bit of a smirk, and then directed me—and the rickshaw—to one of the large garage doors in the complex. I trotted down the road, the door opened, and I was waved in by a stocky guard who at first gave me a broad smile, and then, wiping that away, a firm directive

Joseph Woodcock

to leave the rickshaw in the middle of the building. He then escorted me to a locked room where I sat with several dejected looking souls.

What I did not know was that some new recruits were being trained and being led into the garage to search a rickshaw. Some thought it was a joke or perhaps that it was the start of some hazing ritual. But when I was led out to the garage a few minutes later some seemed relieved that it was not part of a hidden camera episode on a cable network. After an uneventful search, I left the garage. I had to enter a busy highway on my way to the next small town; it was only a few kilometers, but with a state trooper sitting there and my recent experience in Manitoba, I thought it better to ask. The trooper looked at me for a few seconds and gave me a simple nod. With that I thanked him and trotted down the highway and into the small town of Pembina, North Dakota.

It was late morning when I entered Pembina. I had made a decision to do my best to make it to a town each day as I was not sure how US or state law enforcement felt about me just camping on the side of the road. Once I looked at the map and plotted a route for the next week or so, it looked like I would be able to accomplish that. After a cup of coffee and a late breakfast at a local diner, I slipped over the Red River into Minnesota. I had only walked for a few kilometers when a carload of young people showed up and stopped in front of me. A nice young lady was interested in journalism and was spending some time that summer writing for a local paper. She asked a few questions during the interview, but it seemed she had one final request: she wanted to "pull that rickshaw for a spell." It was not an entirely isolated request, as in Canada some people wanted to get a photo of themselves in it, but she wanted to actually feel a bit what it would be like to pull it.

Over the next seven weeks as I travelled through the US two things were constant. The first was that nearly every few days a local newspaper would interview me and every day, without fail, at least one person would ask to pull the rickshaw for a while. Sometimes it was just one kilometer, but most wanted at least thirty minutes under its yoke. Some positioned themselves so they could pull it up a great hill and one man, after seeing a short interview with me on the late local TV news, told his "woman" that he was going to find me the next day.

In the morning he drove his Harley Davidson motorcycle until he passed me and then he drove on at least ten kilometers ahead, parked the bike, and walked back to meet me. Of course, I hadn't noticed him pass me, but I did notice an extra-large biker walking toward me in the middle of nowhere. After some good conversation, he gave me T-shirt from a local endurance race and asked if he could "give that a pull." In the mid-day heat, wearing old jeans and some shit-kicking biker boots, he pulled that rickshaw well past where he had left his bike. And then stopping, thanked me very much. I took his photo and offered to email it to him, but he replied, "What for?"

After leaving Pembina, I rolled into the small settlement of Humbolt in the late afternoon. It was just a small collection of nicely tended houses, though the streets were nearly deserted. I did not see any obvious signs of a structured camping area, so I found the local post office and walked in. I introduced myself to the postmistress and told her how and where I was travelling and asked if there was a spot to set up my tent for the evening. I explained that I would be gone in the morning and would leave no mess. She picked up the phone and called the town clerk and then said I could camp in the local park.

After setting up and having a bit of a nap in the shade I was woken and presented with some supper. This trend continued almost every evening. In all the time I walked though Minnesota, Wisconsin, and Michigan over half of the time when I stopped in a restaurant for coffee or a meal the tab would be paid before I got to the till, and most of the time I did not know whom to thank.

I immediately found that Americans love individualism and respect the spirit of exploration and adventure. In Canada, I was self-sufficient and for the most part just relied on myself,

Joseph Woodcock

but now I had to seek out assistance almost daily regarding something. This bridge not only allowed interaction, but also facilitated networking. It seemed that each meeting would spawn others; when I would ask about the services available in the next town, for example, someone would of course know that information but would also give me personal contacts who, when I arrived, were expecting me. These people for the most part were not businesses or organisations, but just individuals and families that would give me a shady spot under a tree in their yard. Most often I would be brought out a meal and never once did any of them accept any payment for their kindness.

After Humbolt I spent the night in Hallock and attended the local county fair. Afterward, I went on to Bronson Lake State Park and then turned south toward Thief River Falls. At Bronson Lake I was invited to a social around a large campfire and listened to guitar and banjo picking until all hours. There was a terrific storyteller for the kids also, and it all made me think back to a campout when I was young.

Our neighbours had belonged to an organised camping society, which generally was more of a social get-together than anything else. One weekend they had a camping trip planned for the heavily wooded area of the Koksilah River, not far from where we lived, and I was invited. The group, which was large, had been active for many years, so there was a bit of a hierarchy and some of the old members, who generally were retired, had time on their hands.

One of the prize duties of the volunteers was to be part of the giant campfire and storytelling group, which kind of reminded me of a secret society, as everything they did was cloak and dagger. In the daylight, the entire area was roped off and patrolled by Legion members who were also part of the camping group. One could hear sawing and hammering and of course, as dusk fell, most of them were drinking. No one was allowed anywhere near the giant campfire area and secrecy and rumour swirled about the general camping public.

As nightfall came on, a large gong was struck in a slow, haunting rhythm to call the campers to the central area. The trails to the

keremeye'us

fire were kind of eerie as we walked single-file from all reaches of the forest toward a beckoning light and an ancient drum. The thick West Coast forest was a tangle under massive, crooked red cedar trees and one felt that at any second a claw might reach out and pull you into the darkness. Once at the large circle there was food and entertainment, but the dancing flames against the giant walls of timber kept all the kids—there seemed to be about a hundred of us—away from the toilets, which were within the darkness.

Then the storytelling began and it was impressive in its sheer terror. Some of the old men, dressed in garb, would walk between the giant trees so that the light of the fire just touched them. Others screamed and rustled bushes in time with the storyteller's script. The old men had run a propane gas line under the dirt from somewhere on the edge of the woods to under the fire pit; when the storytellers asked for a sign that something terrible was going to happen that night to the children, flames burst upward. We were freaking out—It was a truly nightmarish effect.

It was a time when sasquatch sightings were all the rage and the movie The Legend of Boggy Creek was showing in town, so the storytellers had created an "abduction by sasquatch" theme. Already near hysteria, the kids clung to each other as a slow, haunting growl echoed through the forest. The retirees had found that if you take an oversized empty coffee can and drill a small hole in the metal end, a piece of twine pulled though that hole slowly produces growl. And, if you pull it quickly the growl becomes a howl.

So it was with this invention that the retirees induced terror into the souls of the young. Several groups of them in the woods encircling the fire area would turn the open ends up or away so that the grunts and growls, and then the long terrifying howls, echoed and stretched throughout the forest. "They have come," the storytellers pronounced, "and some of you will be devoured this night." It was beyond any rules of entertainment as kids were crying and were inconsolable. Then the storytellers said, "The only way to avoid the jaws of the beast is to hide in the river as the beasts hate the water," and with that a couple of kids ran into the timber toward the river. I don't know if they were part of the script, maybe dwarfs or midgets, but no one went after them. I don't know what happened to them, maybe the current took them away; I was just sitting there frozen, sucking my thumb.

Later that night, with all the parents into the homemade wine and the kids having nightmares in their tents, one of the old guys, who did not know when to stop, began that growling and howling next to of some of the pup tents and a few of the kids, their bladders packed with cream soda but too scared to go out to pee, wet their pants in terror.

The weather around Thief River Falls became a mix of light rain and blustery conditions, so I took a couple of days there before moving south to Red Lake Falls and then east again on the slow climb toward Bemidji. The area around Bemidji is the headwaters for the Mississippi River, the home of the giant statues of Paul Bunyan and his bull Blue, and an incredible recreation area. I stayed two days before crossing the Mississippi on my trek to Duluth. Each day, from when I crossed the Mississippi to the end of the season a month later, I ate fresh fish as it was inexpensive and offered everywhere. Each restaurant or tavern boasted walls of gigantic freshwater trophies to marvel at, along with history rich and deep.

After passing through the famed Chippewa National Forest I bought supplies at Grand Rapids in preparation for a few days of relative isolation. The expanse between Grand Rapids and Duluth runs along a great break of land; the waters on one side run to the Gulf of Mexico and on the other side, to Lake Superior and then the Atlantic Ocean. Near Savanna Portage State Park one can almost feel the apprehension and fear as peoples long before us dragged their canoes from waters and lands known to currents of another world. After several long days of travel and in heavy rains, I edged over the ridge and descended down into Duluth at the head of Lake Superior. It was a magnificent sight.

I only spent one night in Duluth and thought I would spend another just over the bridge in Superior, Wisconsin. After asking around I found that there are two bridges that cross the wide divide, but only one allows foot traffic. I woke to a terribly hot day and with the last few days of rain, the humidity was crazy—just getting the rickshaw back together and packed was laborious. I had a few things to buy, had a late breakfast, and then read the local paper.

Almost the entire newspaper was centered on one main subject, the same subject I had been reading about for days and dominated the TV News the night before. It seems that starting that day and for the entire weekend, Duluth and Superior were hosting two rival biker gangs who were essentially at war with one another. Everyone seemed to have an opinion about what would take place, ranging from an all-out bloodbath to nothing at all. All the scenarios centered on if one group or the other tried to cross one of the bridges, so all law enforcement were on high alert with extra staff being called in on both the local and state levels. Hundreds of ill-tempered bikers roared up and down each side of the bay, most likely trying to find a Walmart or a Krispy Cream. However, the news machine was going mad interviewing people on the street and instigating hysteria.

I got lost in the paper, so by the time I actually thought about crossing over, it was near noon. Because of the sharp grades above Duluth, the ramps to the bridge dive down steep into the old part of the city, so once down on street level it is hard to get your bearings on which ramp to take. I found an Information Center, strolled in and asked an extremely personable young lady which ramp to take to walk onto the bridge to cross over to Superior. Now I don't know what came over me, but as she started to talk, I simply did not listen. She even drew a small map, but I just could not wait for her to stop talking and when she did, I quickly folded up the small map, placed it in my bag, thanked her, and walked out the door not knowing any more than when I walked in.

She had said for me to make a left but as soon as I exited the door I started pulling the rickshaw to the right, up a ramp that was right there and had a sidewalk and everything. So up and around I trotted on the painted sidewalk as it dodged between

Joseph Woodcock

pillars and other ramps until all the ramps converged into one main multi-lane deck. As it did, the painted sidewalk came to an end at a large concrete abutment. It was, perhaps, three feet high and on top of it was a six-foot chain-link fence and, for proper measure I think, some razor wire as well. Behind all of this was the walkway over the bridge.

The walkway came up on another ramp and was, as far as I could see, caged the entire way and impossible to climb over empty-handed, never mind with a rickshaw and two hundred pounds of gear. It was obvious that I was on the wrong ramp, so I took a few minutes to weigh my options. I really had no option other than to go back and around as the walkway was on the other side of this Berlin Wall, and no matter how long I stood there looking irritated, it was not going to come down. To go back down the ramp I came up and walk the few blocks to the correct ramp and then walk back up to where I was would have taken about fifteen minutes. Of course, I did not have that kind of time, so with nowhere I needed to be and months to accomplish it, I stared at the bridge deck as traffic swirled in from all sides at high speeds.

It did not look that far. I somehow let this become an option and stood there, my stomach bloated with a big American breakfast, which included three eggs, three types of meat, grits, beans, toast and jam and peanut butter, and more coffee than Colombia. I mean just standing there I was sweating and panting with the heat and humidity. On the fence in front of me was posted a list of federal, state, and local laws forbidding anyone walking on this bridge other than in the caged walkway. But did this mean me? Who were they talking to? And so I pondered for another moment and then I bolted into the traffic.

On either side of the bridge, tucked away in vacant lots and alleys, hidden from public so as to not panic anyone, were brigades of law enforcement officers ready to act if either biker group decided to cross. The senior officer was caught off guard when the dispatcher informed him that a man was "running on the bridge" and then he thought he heard the word "rickshaw." Quickly thinking the word "rickshaw" was a code word for something spectacular, like "Broken Arrow" or "Mincemeat," two cars from each side blasted onto the bridge deck, sirens and lights ablaze.

I could hear them coming and even though I already felt like I had run most of the way, I had actually only begun, and the traffic, clearly overreacting, laid on their horns and swerved out of the way in great wide turns, cutting off others who in turn jammed on their brakes. It was instant insanity. I just knew some were fumbling around in the glove box for their pistols while big ladies in beehive hairdos barked out threats and freckled youth banged on car windows. Thankfully, two state trooper cars pulled in behind me, one blocking the lane I was in and the other blocking the next lane, leaving just one lane where a moment before there were three. Traffic instantly came to a standstill.

As I stared into the mirrored sunglasses of the state trooper, I just started talking. In one continuous sentence, which seemed as long as the bridge itself, I tried to blame the whole thing on the girl who gave me the stupid directions. Slandering and mocking her, I pulled out the map she had drawn me as if to show the officers how ambiguous and vague her directions were. Unfolding it with a sneer I was dumbstruck to see a map of both incredible detail and simplicity. It had the Information Center and then each turn with street numbers with little arrows easily directing me to the ramp I had inquired about.

Also, it showed a little bit of the route I did take and she had drawn a small sad face there and the words "Not this way." Quickly stuffing the map in my shirt I was thinking of stories I could tell to avoid being pistol-whipped. The officer was looking at me for a long time before I blurted out that I was Canadian and was "travelling this majestic land" and "pretty cool ride I have, eh? Want to pull it for a while?" My knees were actually knocking and the entire big American breakfast was rolling over in my stomach. It was clear I was going down.

With cross-border trade principally at a halt, the trooper told me to get back in "that thing" and start running. He was going to drive right behind me with lights on and the other car would be a little farther back and they were going to escort me to the other side. With my little legs already rubber and what felt like a hair dryer on high in my face, I wanted to correct his impression that I ran in the rickshaw when I actually just walked. Before I could raise this point he was in his car and nudging me up the bridge deck. Running in the rickshaw is like doing the one hundred yard hurdle dash in a tight hoop skirt, but with two state troopers and a hundred or so honking cars behind me, I was motivated to do so. I could see the crest of the bridge in the distance, but with the heat and the weight of the big American breakfast as additional burdens, it seemed to be moving away at times.

I just kept thinking that once I crested the rise things would be better, but as I reached the top it seemed to me that the expectation was for me to speed up and within seconds I was primarily in a controlled crash. My legs were sort of dangling from my hips as the two hundred pounds of supplies felt the grasp of gravity and tried to surge over me. The faster I went the faster it went and so I just tried to keep it straight and not trip or stumble, because at this speed the rickshaw would run me over entirely.

As I tried to concentrate on staying aloft I heard a voice beside me. Looking over I saw an entire family in an exceedingly long SUV pulling a multi-axle travel trailer. They had their windows down and a woman was videoing me and talking about how thrilling it was that I was running across America. Her husband, leaning way over her and now crowding me closer to the cement abutment, was going on about their being from Kentucky. He began to introduce his wife and the three kids in the back and explained that he had an older son but he was in military college somewhere, and on it went. I am sure we were doing forty miles an hour.

The state troopers started flipping their sirens and horns

keremeye'us

off and on and then began to issue firm directives with the loud speaker for the Kentucky family to move on. The driver, now fully turned around in his seat to look back at the commotion, edged even closer to the right and I tried to scream at him, but nothing came out. I am not sure if it was the river of sweat flowing down my face or one of the kids with a squirt gun, but my left eye filled with fluid and with my right eye having only very limited vision, suddenly I felt as though I was looking through an ice cube.

It seemed as though I was in the middle of a capsule re-entry, a violent and dangerous free-fall with the landing area bouncing and shaking wildly back and forth from one side of my peripheral vision to the other. Edging forward, the Kentuckians were seamlessly replaced by the roar of several Harleys. In my half-blind state I thought that one of the biker groups formed an assault line behind me with the rickshaw being the sharp point of the dagger. But it was worse than that—it was eight or ten retirees from Redding, California, all jostling and bobbing with their "hogs" to get a memory for their video diaries. I was thinking, "What the fuck next, a combine?"

The state trooper pushed them forward and took a flanking position to my immediate rear giving me some room. I was gasping for air, weaving sporadically and randomly as if I was a pinball between the abutment and the white line, when the end of the bridge came into view. Digging deep, I tried to concentrate, the girders drumming by as blades of a fan until the arc above me fragmented away and I was free of it. Tragically, though, unlike the ramps on the Duluth side, which fall into the town, the ramps of the Superior side wandered aimlessly together for some distance from the bridge deck. Now, with my entire left side seemingly paralysed and my lungs heaving, the big American breakfast catapulted forward. I could see spots flutter and then pop as incandescent bubbles as I thrashed about trying to pull the burden the last few meters up hill.

Lunging between the blocks of cement, I tripped on the curb and allowed the rickshaw to settle on top of me, just clear

Joseph Woodcock

of the ramp. Convulsions and tremors overtook me and I flailed about trying to hold on as if the earth was spinning wildly. Somehow I located my water bottle but after snapping off the cap and holding it vertically, only a thimbleful of water trickled down my throat. The trooper was beside me and was now asking questions. Unable even to compute what he was saying, I barked out like a seal, unable to construct even one word. Whatever I managed to communicate, he seemed alright with it, as he slipped into his cruiser and sped away. After laying in that spot for some time, I found some shade beside a dumpster and in untying my two canvas water storage sacks from the rickshaw, drank the contents of one and poured the other over my head. I was now in Wisconsin, the Dairy State.

I found a small motel and spent the afternoon sitting in a lawn chair on the beach, marvelling at the expanse of Lake Superior in front of me. A few hours later, while enjoying a fabulous meal, outdoor music sifted over the district and I drank in the atmosphere and laughter around me. As darkness fell, so did I, and I collapsed into my bed almost as fast as I could—painfully—get my clothes off.

In the brisk early morning, I edged a bit south and then eastward again through the vast recreation area along the south shore of Lake Superior. Every day I enjoyed the fabulous people of this region and every night slept under silent skies. Stopping in Ashland, I crossed into Michigan at Ironwood and then into the granite hills before the steady descent into Marquette. It had been three weeks of steady travel and though the conditions were impossible to beat, I was looking forward to some rest.

As I neared Marquette I was interviewed by the local newspaper and again by the local television news station. After spending just one night camping at the municipal park I searched out a good restaurant for some breakfast and savoured both the food and the atmosphere. The restaurant was full, and now, with my photo and story in the morning paper and the piece on the late night TV news, people chatted back and forth with me as I ate. After breakfast, I enjoyed a pleasant

keremeye'us

conversation with the restaurant owners before sliding under the canopy of the rickshaw and walking away. August was waning and I made the decision to end the current season in Sault Ste. Marie, perhaps ten days away.

Leaving Marquette, I strolled along its lakeshore boardwalk and then along the beach road. I happened upon an elderly woman who was in her bathrobe and was taking the newspaper from her mailbox. She turned, a little startled to see me, but we wished each other a good morning and carried on, each on our way. Not long afterward a car crawled up behind me and as I turned I saw it was the same woman. She stopped, got out of the car, and walked over to me carrying a package.

She said that after seeing me this morning at the end of her driveway she sat down for her coffee and saw the photo of me and read the story of my walk. After reading it, she could not stop herself from getting dressed and meeting with me in person. After a few minutes of chit chat, she handed me the package and opening it I found a small flag. She said, "My husband, whom I miss dearly, died some time ago. He was an employee of the State for many years and at his funeral I was presented with this flag of the State of Michigan for his service. He was a wonderful person who would have loved to talk with you. I have been looking at this flag for a long time and always wanted to do something meaningful with it. After reading the article this morning, I instantly knew what he would want. That is why I am asking you to take this flag with you so that he can witness and experience the simple and pure pleasures of your journey." Overcome with emotion, I thanked her for her generous gift. We stood there for a long time as I searched for some words, but in the end she thanked me again, turned, and drove away.

For a few more days I followed the sandy shore and then, turning inland, I climbed up onto the tablelands of the Upper Peninsula. Heading almost straight east from Shingleton I was able to find a room and bath each night and spent my days thinking about the months, and miles past. How fortunate I was to have this opportunity. As I crossed over lazy rivers I was told these were the haunts of the young Hemmingway, who often ventured from the south to fish these waters. Silent and still, some days I would drink my tea and gaze into the distance, watching the surface ripple or flex. Perhaps he had stood right there and cast across the same silent waters. Perhaps he did still.

Walking into Sault Ste. Marie, Michigan, I looked just across the river to its Canadian twin. The skies had opened up and the warm summer rain collapsed upon me. I took shelter in a gas station and enjoyed a coffee and a large chocolate bar while I marvelled at the deluge, feeling content just to sit. As the afternoon crept into evening, the rain stopped and I crossed over to the Canadian side. The next morning I packed my gear and sent it west as freight and then stepped on a plane for the short flight home. It had been a terrific walk so far and even as I flew west, I looked forward to the spring and the continuation of the journey.

keremeye'us

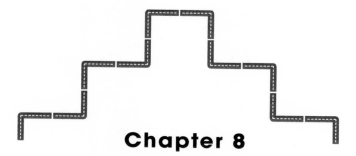

Chapter 8

I spent the winter working as a camp handyman in northern Alberta. I had made some small changes to the rickshaw, adding some things and removing others, but in the end the net weight was close to the same. After seven months of winter, I was again ready to feel the open spaces and the taste of adventure. I landed in Sault Ste. Marie, picked up my gear from the freight company, and the very next morning pulled out of town. Of course, I tried to limit the distance each day so I could again adjust to the physical demands, but as I enjoyed the time so much I found this hard to do. The first week is critical as any small injuries incurred then can hamper and nag at you for weeks. With this in mind, and also because the weather was still chilly, I found a room anytime I could and nursed any sores.

Along the north shore of Lake Huron I pulled into a small bed and breakfast and, after finding something to eat, took a walk out on the breakwater. As I stood there taking in the view, an orange cat wrapped itself around my ankles and I bent down and gave it a good scratching. It instantly reminded me of a cat Kitten and I had as a young married couple.

We had been married a couple years and had just purchased

a house, but did not have any children yet. Someone gave us a little orange kitten. It was always under our feet, constantly meowed in a begging fashion, and after a couple weeks it was wearing a bit on both of us. My brother George was staying in our basement and had decided to go cold turkey on booze and cigarettes and was having, as one can imagine, a difficult time of it. Kitten, who was a fabulous cook, made a big Sunday night dinner, most likely turkey or ham with all the fixings. As she set the table I called George up from the basement. George loved a tasty meal and lavished praise on Kitten for the feast. When we had finished eating, George insisted on doing all the dishes and he shuffled the two of us into the living room to have tea and relax. So, with Kitten and I watching the evening news, George started to clean up.

The house was our first and we lacked some furniture and the kitchen itself was unusually long and fairly narrow. At the far end a kitchen nook should have sat, but we did not yet have the funds for adding one; this added to the length of unimpeded space. As George started to clean up, Ope the kitten was instantly at his feet, sure he was going to get some scraps. As George cleared the table, Ope was continuously tripping him up and, throughout every step, meowed loudly and darted under his feet.

This went on and on and the whole time George, who was now craving a cigarette or a drink, started to become agitated. He leaned down and opened the dishwasher and Ope tried to climb inside; the cat was in and out of the lower cupboards and under George's feet, all the time meowing out in painful wails of hunger. Back to the table went George and like a loose shoelace, the cat flipped and flopped around his ankles and the aggravating purring and mewing elevated.

George's frustration grew—he felt like his skin was crawling. He placed some glasses in the top cupboard and leaned down to reach into the dishwasher. Ope was instantly under George's feet again and, now bent over, George was pivoting around the dishwasher door just trying to get some peace. At his wits end, George lifted his head quickly and smashed the back of his skull on the bottom door of the cupboard that he had just left open.

Joseph Woodcock

Kitten and I heard the loud crash as George's head hit and we rose up quickly to run into the kitchen. We came in behind George who had staggered back to the table. George did not see us, but was transfixed on Ope, who was sitting in the middle of the floor. Blind with anger, George took three long steps and, like a fifty-yard field goal attempt, booted Ope the entire length of the kitchen. The wee orange fluff sailed through the air and slammed hard into the wall near where it met the ceiling.

On several levels and only for perhaps a second, George's pain went away as the kick was solid and Ope's impact hard. But as the orange corpse slid down the wall, Kitten who loved that cat, cried out "Ope!" She burst into tears, ran to the now motionless ginger waif, and threw herself on the floor. George, feeling the impact and weight of his actions, wailed out and, Quasimodo-like, ran past her and down the steep stairs to the dark basement.

It was all too much for George as he slipped away into the night to find a drink. For Ope though, he was all right and life was extremely enjoyable for him for another nine months. The kitchen incident sparked a nurturing hormone within Kitten, whom we did not know at the time was just pregnant, and Ope was showered with affection and love. Ope had cat toys, cat beds, cat obstacle climbs, and even cat treats for just being a cat. Ope never went outside, slept all day, licked his nuts, and if he was near the litter box, he sometimes shit in there—sometimes.

But the end of Ope's reign was near. When we walked through the front door with our new daughter, Kitten's mother threw the cat out onto the middle of the lawn where he stood frozen for some time, unable to grasp what had just occurred. Other than peering in through a rain-soaked window, Ope never again saw the inside of the house.

Not that we were paying any attention after that, but Ope's health began deteriorating at a steady rate as he was relegated to some sort of "cat gang bitch" and spent most of his time hiding under the woodpile. Fearing he was to be curb-stomped by the other cats, Ope stuck to the shadows and only reappeared to quickly run out and eat his dry cat food.

keremeye'us

Then he went through an extended phase of standing on top of the woodpile, hissing and snarling continuously. His eyes were wide open, as he was too scared even to blink. Even though he was eating, he was skin and bones and mange had set in; at two years old, Ope looked like a dishrag. Then one day, I went to put Ope's food out at the regular time and there waiting patiently for me was a forty-pound mother racoon. It seems that in the last six months or so Ope had lived on grasshoppers. The racoon, I found out later, was terrorizing the neighbourhood, eating all the pet food and brutalizing any dogs or cats in her way.

The neighbours later told me that once challenged by a pure-bred giant poodle, the mother racoon stopped momentarily, then tore off its face before completing her rounds. Standing there holding the bag of cat food, I was thinking what measures I could take to rid Ope of the racoon terror. Before I could come up with a solution I was distracted—baby Jessica farted or smiled and, hearing Kitten's elation, I threw the food out onto the step and slammed the door.

I was feeling the physical discomforts of the first week of walking as I neared the town of Espanola. I met a couple about ten kilometers from town who later rode back out to invite me over for the evening. Both were retired bike enthusiasts who had pedaled through parts of Europe. We had a good evening and the next day I set out for Manitoulin Island. I stopped at White Fish Falls, camped across from a local pub, and enjoyed a splendid meal there.

Since the ferry I was going to catch to the Bruce Peninsula was seasonal and not yet in operation, I spent two nights in Little Current and travelled slowly to South Baymouth. Manitoulin Island is quiet that time of the year and the narrow roads winding through the mixed forests seem so composed and steady. It was that moment between winter and spring when plans are projected but not yet made, and waters, though still, are months from being warm. The cabins and cottages were still silent under the naked maples but soon would be filled with laughter and games. It reminded me of our small

Joseph Woodcock

cabin at Swansea, near Sicamous, British Columbia.

My father had built the simple structure at Mara Lake and each summer, when I was very young, was spent at the cabin. There were so many kids there, between all the cabins and all the campers the woods and beaches were overrun. One afternoon my cousin Terry and I were alone in the cabin playing. My older brother Mike and his buddy Glen thought it would be fun to scare us. Glen stole a white sheet from his mother's linen supply and Mike threw this over his head and then began to negotiate the gravel road toward our cabin.

Hearing ghostly noises, Terry and I—we were only about five years old—looked out the window to see the presence coming up the road. She was scared, so I jumped to the rescue and pulled a hefty chunk of firewood from the wood box and waited at the door. My brother Mike came down the walkway and was having difficulty placing his feet on the small step. I opened the door and with Mike concentrating on his footing, I slammed the dry birch log over his head. There were a few seconds of silence before I heard Glen running away and, looking down, I saw a large red stain forming on the sheet.

Only half-knowing what happened, I grabbed Terry and we ran to the beach and sat in a lawn chair with everyone else enjoying the evening around us. Across from us was Glen, who, if found out, would get a beating from his mother for the sheet, so his silence was complicit. So we sat there pretending all was well but up the road, at the bottom of the step lay my brother Mike, his head split wide open. It was terrific fun.

A few weeks later there were several days of wet weather. With the irritation of kids hanging about the cabin waiting for the weather to change, my mother continuously threatened us if we got our jeans wet. Our cabin was just across the lane from the beach, but if we were wearing our clothes and decided to go swimming that couple hundred feet seemed too far and often we would just dive in, clothes and all. This killed my mother as the tiny cabin had no services and it meant unnecessary extra work for her. It was one of her triggers and if you came home wet in your clothes you had to

keremeye'us

be prepared for the consequences.

One dreary wet morning I walked across the road wearing my street clothes and a light jacket and, finding the beach empty and most still asleep, I skipped some stones and poked at the water with a long stick. I stepped up onto the wharf and walked back and forth its long length, dragging the tip of the stick in the water. In a complete daydream, I walked right off of the end of the pier. Of course I could swim, but I was only five years old, and when I came up I was under the wharf. My clothes were heavy and I panicked, struggling to get out, but in my desperation I had moved farther away from the edge of the wharf. My jacket rose up over my head; I felt entangled and began to feel the pull downward as my lungs filled with water. I felt myself slipping away. My legs would not kick and I began to sink.

A boy just a couple years older than me had seen me on the wharf and then he noticed that I was gone and he wondered if it was an illusion. He came out of his parents' cabin and suspiciously paced the length of the pier as the wind churned the surface of the lake. He stood for a moment and looked about; he could hear his mother calling and felt the light rain in his face and he turned to her and began to walk. As he did, he stepped over the stick and the snapshot of it in my hand flashed in front of him. He reached into the waters along the edge of the slippery pier and caught some fabric. He tugged at it and a body emerged.

There was only silence, I remember. A numbing and distant sensation that I was there, but apart, severed from my skin. He tried to pull me up and his screams emptied the cabins as the people rushed to the shore. The dock sank from the weight as men and boys grappled to secure and then to retrieve me. They rolled my limp body to my side and directed a solid knee to my back, and then did it again. The water erupted from my lungs.

I screamed and heaved and became hysterical, but once I was helped to my feet I instantly began to walk home. Some boys were with me and then, behind them, a few more. As a funnel, a procession of parents and friends followed me across the road, everyone stunned with regard to what had just happened. My mother, who

Joseph Woodcock

was doing dishes at the sink, heard the crying and, peering out a bit, saw me walking toward the cabin, crying and soaking wet.

My mother thought that I had gone swimming in my clothes and she saw only red. Not even noticing the crowd of concerned and awestruck neighbours, she swung open the door and came at me. I was about halfway down the walk and had increased my howling as I neared the door. It opened and my mother, a cigarette in her lips and her right arm in the air, shuffled sideways on her feet for the distance between us and slapped me as hard as she could to the ground. "I told you to never go swimming in your clothes, ya daft wee bastard," she yelled. She continued on for a sentence or two before looking up to the stunned stare of the neighbourhood, standing frozen on the road just a few feet away.

Lost to as why everyone was even there and, even more so, confused with the look of horror on their faces, my mother tried to piece together the fragments. Then they all barked out that Joey had essentially just come back from the dead and in sharp detail explained how I was rescued and revived. Like Ope, in the time after George had punted him the full length of the kitchen, I had a short period in which I enjoyed some memorable treatments—in a family of seven kids the near drowning was worth it.

Crossing from South Baymouth to Tobermory on the first day of the operating season, I enjoyed a day of easy travel. Once to the shore of the Bruce Peninsula I decided to spend the night in a small motel. A terrific rainstorm was crossing over the area and I spread my maps over the table, nursed a tea, and looked ahead. The pace over the previous two weeks had been perfect and with clearing skies, I looked forward to the rural countryside ahead.

In the morning, I first enjoyed a delightful coffee overlooking the narrow harbour and then slipped again southward. In the weeks ahead I nudged along the steady rise of the Niagara Escarpment. I stopped for lunch one afternoon at a roadside diner at Dundalk, the highest elevation population centre in Ontario. Looking out over the farmland, I thought back to just a year prior when I struggled over the icy pass of the Rocky

Mountains; it seemed like it was so long ago. The people of this area were so friendly and it seems most of my days were spent just leaning against an old truck chatting with the locals. I began to edge eastward and slipped past Lake Simcoe and, after camping for several days in the oak forests, headed south again to Oshawa and Lake Ontario.

I love history and, starting on the north shore of Lake Ontario, I walked from one museum to another, drinking in as much of the past as possible. I read a great deal of the St. Lawrence and its arterial importance and I marvelled at the contributions and staggering chronological pace in which it drew the brave and desperate to its shores. I had always said that I would like to take a walking holiday and the two months ahead, right to the stone walls of Quebec City, would prove to be just that. It was to become a perfect mix of travel and relaxation.

I camped on the grassy shore near Brighton and was washed by the warm breeze off the lake. The temperatures were now rising and the forecast for the next two weeks was brilliant. I was not supposed to camp there, but those who walked quietly by gave me a nod and a smile. Into the evening I just sat and from distant dunes shorebirds dropped and darted, swirling in formations tight and swift. I thought of the days we had spent together, my brother and I, walking coastal shores such as these.

My brother was attending college in Nanaimo and I would hitchhike up to see him. After nights of superb music on the stereo and conversations that covered politics and economy, poetry and song, Mike and I would rise in the early mornings and make heavy sandwiches of block cheese and onion, fill our thermoses with mint tea, and drive his Austin Mini into the morning rains.

He was far more than a brother to me. Though a few years older, he included me always, even under the taunt of his friends. My brother always had room for me. In the years of torment and isolation as the last shards of our family came apart, my brother would find me late at night and together we would walk for hours, sometimes until dawn, in the soft Pacific rains. I always felt valued

Joseph Woodcock

by him, my opinion mattered, and no matter what the subject, he allowed me to contribute. As they say, it is just the simple things that keep hope from slipping away.

It was enough. He always had faith and a blind belief in me; he told me to quit school and looking me in the eyes said, "You are too smart for it." Of course, I was not too smart, but he recognised that if I did not find sanctuary soon, it would be too late. Alcoholism had completely destroyed any sense of family or home and I struggled daily to cope.

When I was young, a cat wandered into our yard. With the animal shelter just down the road, it was common to have people just tie their unwanted pets to the gate rather than paying the fees to take them in. This large tabby cat had somehow managed to free himself and was dragging his leash behind when I coaxed him onto my lap. After some petting, I sat the cat down and went into the house to get him some milk but in returning I found him gone. His disappearance was a small mystery, but one that was shuffled to the side quickly.

A month later, as the leaves were starting to fall, my parents and I turned off of the road and into our driveway. It was hard to see at first, but my father pointed out something hanging in the high branches of the maple tree behind the garage. As we stopped it was clear that it was the tabby cat. We surmised that he had climbed up there after I sat him down and he had become tangled. He hung there by his neck, the braided leash still clipped to the speckled collar.

It was an image that I repeatedly woke up to over the years. It was not one of horror or fear, but one that seemed to draw me in. The tabby cat seemed at peace there, framed by the turning colours of the leaves. Somehow, his bulging eyes and open jaws beckoned me, invited me and compared to my fear and torment, his fate seemed at times, less of an option and more of a solution.

More than anyone or anything, it was my brother Mike whom I saw as I struggled with the image of the tabby cat. We never talked of it and I wondered if he knew. He always seemed to be there when I needed him most. He was pragmatic and focused and I felt that

keremeye'us

that solution would disappoint him. Though I always saw the tabby cat's fate as an option, my brother Mike never let it become a final solution. His faith and conviction in me was like a drug.

I had secured a summer job in Nanaimo for the Fish and Wildlife Branch so Mike and I rented a seasonal cabin along the river. Mike was working away logging for the most part and did not need a place and though he paid the vast majority of the rent, the space was for me. For the first time, my life was predictable. I cannot express the feeling of self-confidence that summer gave me. At seventeen, I spun that summer job into a one-year contract, working with the information and education officers of the Branch. In the fall, we gave up the cabin and I moved into the city. That first winter on my own was difficult, but I looked forward to every day and as time passed was proud of my accomplishments. More than anything, I was grateful to my bother.

Some days along the St. Lawrence River it seems I barely travelled. I could sit on the bluffs and watch the ships all day. But as the weeks came and went I moved steadily east and one day, almost by surprise, I walked into Cornwall. I had pegged Cornwall as a possible pivot, thinking possibly of heading into New York State and perhaps the eastern US seaboard. So I took a couple of days to think it over, but it was clear that I was addicted to the great river. So, pulling out my French phrase guide, I again was carried by the river's flow.

On my final day in Ontario, I awoke to heavy rains and cold conditions. I was not acclimatised to this as the weeks prior I had basked in sunshine, so before leaving Cornwall I phoned ahead and reserved a room at a small inn near the Quebec border. Knowing this was waiting for me I shuffled along in the pouring rain and as I neared the small town I was soaking wet and just thinking of a bath. A small line of volunteer fire trucks passed me and an hour later I arrived at the hotel, just in time to see their crews mopping up.

The owner said it started in the kitchen and though I was out a room for the night, it was little compared to the day he'd had. Moving on, I walked into the early evening and found what

Joseph Woodcock

looked like an abandoned motel across from a gas bar. I asked the south Asian man if it was open and he phoned his wife who came down to get me a room. It had been one of those all-inclusive truck centres at one time with fuels, rooms, a bar, and probably gaming, but an adjustment to the access from the main highway a few years back had isolated it from the traffic flow. Anyway, it was clean and had a wicked tub, so I sank into the bubbles and studied my French.

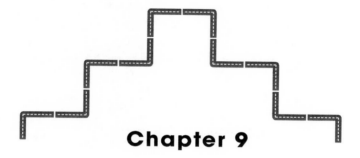

Chapter 9

In the morning I decided to walk the ten kilometers to a small town just inside Quebec. I was craving bacon and eggs, so went over my French-English dictionary and was confident that I would meld right in with the locals. It was still pouring with rain, but I made it to a great restaurant at mid-morning and was almost giddy at the prospect of ordering my meal in French. Right away a beautiful young lady came over to serve me and I ordered up a coffee, toast, potatoes, bacon, and eggs. She wrote that down and I noticed she smiled a bit, but before I could wrap my head around that, she asked how I would like my eggs prepared and then she smiled again.

I had not thought of that, so I we struggled together but in the end got through it. So, with my coffee in front of me, I went back to what I ordered and, though it took some time, I realised that along with my coffee, toast, potatoes, and bacon, I had specified "chicken eggs" as if in Quebec they might slip in "pigeon eggs" instead. Then I laughed as when she asked how I wanted my eggs cooked, she specified "chicken eggs" maybe thinking I would catch on, but I did not. So we had a terrific chuckle when my breakfast arrived as I thanked her for the "chicken eggs." So much for melding right in.

Almost immediately after I entered Quebec I was struck at the vast network of multi-use paths, which are so well-kept and maintained. As I neared Montreal, much of the day was spent along these quiet trails. I was a little apprehensive about walking through Montreal, so I got a small room just before crossing the bridge onto the island itself. I bought a city map and plotted out my route downtown, which I quickly found would primarily be along the Lachine Canal and consisted of either walking paths or quiet residential roads.

The next day was one for the books as I crossed over to the island early and spent the entire day strolling along the waterfront and canal into the centre of Montreal. I had my coffees and lunch in small cafes along the shoreline and took in several outdoor free performances. The people were fantastic. They were curious about the rickshaw and a bit stunned that I had walked from the West Coast. The only thing I had to watch for was that at the end of the business day so many pedal bikes and runners came out of the downtown districts onto the Lachine paths on their way home that I, going against the flow, had to step off for an hour. But it was exciting to see the thousands stream by.

I pulled up from the waterfront and took a seat at an outdoor restaurant. I ordered a large meal as the boulevard came alive with tourists and couples out for an evening. Sitting there at a small table along a narrow cobbled street I should have been taking in all the ambience and splendour, but I was not. I became transfixed on the symphony that was taking place at the restaurant just across the way. It was, from my experiences, an upscale establishment, but for Montreal it was just another delightful place to eat in the midst of thousands of others.

Still, it was a beehive of activity and though it was not quite full, the impression was that it was bustling. The waiters and staff whisked around like humming birds, in and out of the kitchen doors as if controlled by traffic lights; there were no stoppages, but everyone merged together and apart carrying enormous trays of food and drink. "Pop, pop" the corks shot out as a piano filled any void of laughter and conversation. Overpriced food and a snide maître d' only added to the Parisian experience, where one felt privileged just to attend. As I watched all of this I then understood what Mrs. Swanson was desperately trying to accomplish so many years ago.

Mrs. Swanson was one of my teachers in middle school and had an interest in a local restaurant called the Trawler. As the name suggests, it was a seafood eatery, but during her reign it was trying hard to graduate to an exquisite steak and seafood bistro with a strong French-European feel. I do not know what she saw in me, but it seems I looked like genuine dishwasher material because one day she asked me if I wanted to work at the restaurant as a dishwasher and in time, perhaps, I could train for a busboy. Well, I was fifteen years old and even though I was still busy birdwatching on the weekends and working odd jobs, this sounded like something solid.

My brother Mike quickly gave me the book Down and Out in Paris and London by George Orwell, in which the author barely survives as a dishwasher in the less-than-glamorous kitchen dungeons of Europe. So, starting that Saturday afternoon, I rode my bike to the bay and began training. My job entailed some cleaning and helping with the prep cooks first, so I got a terrific idea on how things worked, and the young ladies preparing the side dishes were exceedingly personable and also gave me lots of guidance.

As things came together the servers would show up along with the busboys, bartenders, and finally, right at the last minute, two Paris-trained French Canadian chefs. These two crumbs were all about themselves and barely talked to the prep cooks and certainly would not talk to me. I was, as they called me, a "tas de merde," which sounds a bit poetic, but inherently meant I was a pile of shit. If they wanted something they would shout "plongeur" and point and then mutter something, always ending in some form of "tas de merde."

I just played it up and in the afternoons while helping the prep cooks I would bag up small pieces of vegetables and along with a few partial wine glasses of water, I would hide these behind the dishwasher. In the heat of the battle, when the kitchen was boiling with pressure, I would pretend to be chewing down uneaten food from dirty dishes and drinking wine. They were disgusted and repulsed at what trash was even allowed to be in the next room with them.

My mom loved the stories about those "two fags" as she called them and gave me some half-smoked cigarettes one day. I slipped one into some potatoes on a dirty dish and made a significant scene at finding it and placing it in my pocket. Later, while on break, I fired it up in front of them. "Sac de blu," or something like that—they freaked out and went right to Mrs. Swanson who was kind of freaked out herself as it was actually the only time in two years the two French chefs even acknowledged her existence, and she was the owner. Mrs. Swanson was a bit vague, but even she seemed to sense there was more to it and brushed it off as nonsense.

After months of being a dishwasher, Mrs. Swanson informed me that she was going to start training me for a fill-in busboy. Besides doing some vacuuming, I had not ever been allowed in the dining area and she was so firm on this I thought it even included if we had to evacuate due to a fire. I got to work the first few Saturday afternoons unusually early and the training began. I was surprised to find that even in the ranks of busboy there is a pecking order of duties and all she was training me for at this point was a single duty of delivering chives, bacon bits, and sour cream to customers. I was a bit deflated but soon learned this simplest of tasks requires hours of training.

First was the swinging door. Of course, as we were speaking the swinging door to the kitchen was in a static position, but in the madness when things are rocking, the door is never still. So you can never go out the door unless it is swinging away from you and if you are in the kitchen you stop to wait for it. But if you are in the dining area you must never stop or in any way look as if you are slowing for the swinging door—you must always only enter when it is swinging away from you.

What this meant is that once you are some distance away

from the door you must time your steps to look as if you are not stopping and enter just in time to catch it. "If you were to stop," she said, "...well you must never stop," she added firmly. So for thirty minutes each Saturday Mrs. Swanson would swing the door back and forth and I would leave certain areas of the restaurant and time it so I was swallowed with its motion.

The second item was exiting the swinging door. You could not just walk through the door—you had to "gush." Now, she spent a long time on the word "gush" because, after all, how do you actually "gush" out of a door? What physical motions would one do for someone to say, "Hey, Joe is gushing," other than to perhaps slit my jugular vein, which I was thinking of doing. She meant it in a figurative sense of course, meaning that as the door opened you were to create a presences or a flow. One day I said in error that I was trying to "surge" out of the door and we spent a long time talking about the differences between "surge" and "gush."

Next was the walk. By now I was figuring out where she was going and had watched every episode of Faulty Towers and had become extremely empathetic toward poor Manuel. Also, I was quite light on my feet, so when Mrs. Swanson showed me that I must "float" about the room, I picked it up right away. She never wanted any staff to stand motionless unless performing a task that required it, like pouring wine, which she added, "You will never do... ever!" She said I must take every corner as if it is "banked" and if you are "summoned" to a table to perform your duty and if there is a staff member there you must "divert" and "circle inconspicuously, never stopping" until it is clear, and only then slip in. "Never stand idle. It is a performance out there!" She spoke loudly and then, gaining her composure, repeated the word "performance" softly.

Lastly was my training with the actual condiment container. The one that was used had three small bowls that rotated around a long central handle. It was heavy, even when empty, and was precision-made and balanced on German bearings. Just before I was to gush out of the swinging door I was to give the container a small twirl such that, as I floated about, the three condiments turned slowly. I was only to stop the circular momentum when I

keremeye'us

was actually at the table and only then with the hidden touch of my thumb. I practiced and knew the location of each table so that it would be second nature. I was ready to surge—I mean gush.

The next Saturday with some private school preppy at my station at the dishwasher, I changed into my zoot suit and Mrs. Swanson greased back my hair. Looking in the mirror I could have passed for the younger version of Al Pacino in the movie Scarface. It was a big night as the restaurant was packed and at the central table was a party of twenty celebrating something momentous. I was doing remarkably well and I could see that the initial reaction of Mrs. Swanson was that she had found a diamond in the rough.

As the night revved up, the central table arrived and staff swept about like ice dancers. It was electric, a concert of grace, a performance. I was taking my place near the swinging door, ready for the next command and noticed that the little freak on the dishwasher neglected to add a rinse agent or something. I ridiculed him verbally before uttering a demeaning remark and then with a "gush" caught the motion of the door and banked right into the dining room.

Swerving in and out of the tables the silver condiment server arched and rolled in harmony with my smooth pace. Past the half-wall of the bar, I felt like I was on rails and swept silently, my shoulders and torso linked only as opposing magnets, down the wide runway to the central table. About to arch in, I saw a waitress from somewhere in my peripheral vision react first and so, choking my speed, I circled around the tables at the window and then gingerly performed two figure eights near the piano before floating the final length of the central table to the guest of honour.

Pulling back a little at the end, the condiment tray swept outward and then, for a second hung there as a giant timepiece, before softly settling vertical. As it did, the circular momentum of the tray reached its target speed of one complete turn every two seconds. Sliding back as I approached, the guest of honour now watched as the chives, bacon bits, and then sour cream formed a gentle pirouette in front of him; it was magic and I knew Mrs. Swanson was cheering me on from the shadows.

Joseph Woodcock

I was just about to ask what he preferred when the condiment tray holding the selection fell, hit the edge of the table and flipped over upside down on his lap. Frozen and still holding the tray handle, I stared at his lap as the chives, bacon bits, and sour cream ran together down his crotch. He glared at me, his face beginning to bulge and turn red and I just stood there unable to move. There was a silence and then it was instantly filled with laughter from all the members of the central table, except the guest of honour. I looked at my left hand, still holding just the stem of the tray and put together that the nut on the bottom, holding the German bearings, must have fallen off and the tray simply slipped off.

Then Mrs. Swanson let out a muffled scream and from nowhere and everywhere staff swept in and tried to assist, but I stood as mute as a statue. Mrs. Swanson started apologizing emphatically and going on that it was my first day and that she gave me a chance and what had she been thinking. Between each apology, she turned to me and, with gritted teeth, growled, "You piece of shit" and, "the chefs were right" and then throwing her arms in the air she loudly exclaimed, "What? You never did an equipment check?" as if I just confessed to a crime. I was still holding the stem when it was pried from my fingers and with Mrs. Swanson half whipping me, I was forced back in through the swinging door to the kitchen.

The two chefs, upon hearing the commotion and investigating, simply came apart and rolled between the rows of pots and trays. All food preparation came to an end as sauces boiled over and steaks grew black. Back and forth in front of the swinging door, over and over each of the chefs re-enacted the tragic events and each time they nearly pissed themselves with laughter. Finally, after each one of them did their impression of me being beat back into the kitchen by Mrs. Swanson and the stunned look on my face, some order started to reappear. Fractured it was, though, as every few minutes the entire kitchen staff would start to giggle and then all come apart again. Later I attempted a defense and showed Mrs. Swanson the nut, washer, and German bearings, but it was too late and the next Saturday found myself back at the dishwasher. That

keremeye'us

was the end of my busboy career.

I spend a couple days in Montreal enjoying the sights and then slipped my rickshaw into a storage unit and took the train to Ottawa for the weekend to visit some old friends. Returning again to Montreal I made it off the island the next day and again enjoyed the quiet country roads along the north shore of the river. Though the weather was calm again, I was doing less camping and found myself each night in a quaint auberge. Generally, each auberge had a small restaurant, offered a taste of Europe, and was modestly priced.

By the time I got to Trois-Rivieres I had decided to do a bit of downsizing on my rig. I found a terrific fabrication shop that welded aluminum and had some small changes made, and in the process I sent some equipment back home. I got kind of carried away and included my tent in the shipment and in its place kept a small personal survival tarp, perhaps ten feet square. It was a decision that I would question later on. At the time though, I was looking for more flexibility in choosing tight accommodations in the small settlements, and nothing was sacred.

I was kind of zoned out after that, spending my days strolling along the banks of the river and spending each night enjoying the comforts of the small hotels, but mostly I enjoyed the culture. People were incredibly friendly and open, but I noticed as I approached Quebec City that it became less so. Generally, I would get waves from passing motorists and on the walking paths and lanes people would stop to see what it was all about. I could not quite pin it down—the change I mean—until one Friday morning, just on the outskirts of the city itself.

I was chatting with a young woman who was riding her bicycle and had stopped to talk. As we were conversing she looked a bit uncomfortable and then a car slowed down and a small man started hurling verbal abuse at me. With a putrid glare, he screamed "Hey, anglais" and then something like "bla-bla-bla-bla" and finally ending in some broken English, "you sucker of the cock." He then raced away, all the time waving his arms all about. So I told the young lady that up until a couple of days ago I was well-received but now felt as though people wanted to hurl fish heads at me.

She laughed a bit, realising that I had no idea of why the change had taken place. She asked me if I knew what the date was and of course I did not. She said that starting that day, it was the beginning of Fête Nationale. Of course, I instantly knew the rub as I was flying a Canadian Flag from my rickshaw. She was hesitant to come forward sooner as she thought perhaps I wanted to make a political statement or, as she said, "Perhaps you wanted to die." We had a good laugh and I took down the flag temporarily and replaced it with some ribbon.

I walked through Quebec City that afternoon and took the small ferry across the river to Levis, where I got a room. I spent the entire weekend in the old city taking in the festival—it was a wild time. Once the celebrations were over I started walking eastward along the south shore of the river, which, was now more of a sea. Again, I was back to comforts of the small hotels and superb food.

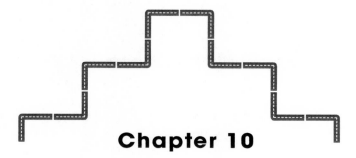

Chapter 10

On a dark and stormy afternoon I took shelter in one of the many large churches of the Quebec townships. With my rickshaw just outside of the wide open doors, I sat in the entrance on a bench and listened to the torrent. Along with the concert of summer rain on hot pavement, giant hardwoods and coastal winds nudged my sentiments and I spent the afternoon taking it all in. With late afternoon approaching, I walked across the path and took a small room overlooking the shallow bay and, listening to the rain through the open window, slept until early evening. A gentle knock at the door suggested it was time for dinner and I took a seat in the corner of the restaurant just down the narrow stairs from my room. I looked across the table at the empty chair and I could see Katie sitting there.

Very soon after we started dating, Katie and I drove to a small family restaurant that one of my coworkers owned. Though the motif then was German, it had much of the same feel as this small restaurant along the wide St. Lawrence. We were served by Rolf, who had suddenly transformed himself from a brash production worker in a factory to a soft-spoken and professional waiter. Katie and I would laugh as we recounted how Rolf had added to the comedy of our first meeting.

Rolf actually had two lives: the one he'd lived in Germany and then the new one after he immigrated to Canada with some of his children. One of his daughters had moved to northern Alberta previously and had been writing letters back to her parents about the wide-open spaces and lack of regulation. Rolf had read the letters, but being born and raised in Germany he doubted the actual validity of his daughter's words. He just thought, her being young, that perhaps she was exaggerating. But her letters persisted and eventually she asked her parents to come to Canada for a visit and see for themselves.

Rolf and his wife agreed and started making preparations for the trip. Once in Edmonton they were to pick up their rental car and then check into the hotel. Then, making sure they have some sort of bag lunch, they were to get up early and drive north toward Smith, then Slave Lake, and finally High Prairie. Rolf's daughter stressed that once they got out of Edmonton they would be driving at least six hours to High Prairie. Rolf scoffed at the information his daughter sent him regarding the time and distances as fiction and he became suspicious.

After landing in Edmonton, Rolf and his wife picked up the car and checked into their room and prepared a lunch for the next day. They rose at dawn and got in the car and followed the signs out of Edmonton. They had travelled for less than two hours but were sure that they had missed High Prairie and became a bit panicky. Pulling into a gas station, they asked the young fellow operating the pumps where they would find High Prairie. He smiled and said continue north for at least four more hours, but they did not have any faith in him, either, and for the next five hours drove around in circles before they headed back to Edmonton and checked back into the same hotel.

They phoned their daughter but she was expecting the call and before they could mount a defense she told them to try and get some sleep and then in the morning get in that God damn car and just do as I have told you. "This is Canada and things are immense here. You will be on gravel roads and you will see deer and moose and maybe bear, as I have told you. So you need to do as I say," their daughter explained again. Rolf did not sleep at all but wondered what transformation or mind-control their daughter was under and what was the purpose of this incredible conspiracy? But after asking everyone in the hotel about directions and all confirming that High Prairie was where they had been told, Rolf asked himself, "Can they all be in on it?" So in the morning they rose and got in the car and drove and drove, neither speaking a word to each other until they came to the Athabasca River. Astonished that the river was where the map said it would be, they stood there stunned until Rolf's wife asked, "Rolf, can they move a river?"

I asked Rolf years later, "Were there not signs on the road indicating where you guys were?" Rolf laughed and said, "Yes, but signs can be moved and maps altered." In disbelief, I asked, "Why would that happen?" Rolf nodded slowly and answered, "During the war, all signs were turned and maps altered." I said to Rolf, "But there was no war at that time," to which Rolf replied, "Seemingly," as if that information also was potentially false. Though Rolf could laugh at his first encounter with Canada, he still held a deep suspicion of most things that he did not totally understand.

One Monday morning I received a call from the office across the street that I could start to send over my crew one or two at a time for testing. "Testing?" I asked, and was reminded that all the employees had to start getting annual pulmonary testing and that an email had been sent out (which I never read). I was mad at myself for not reading the email and I was also angry that I did not get in an extra person or two to take up the work as each person went for the testing. So, while it was mayhem, we were managing.

Just when I needed every person I had to be at their workstations, Rolf was in my office asking what kind of testing was it and what kind of information was needed and what will they do with the information and who are "they?" It went on and on as Rolf, just short of his retirement, felt that this was an elaborate ruse to mine information and use it against him, perhaps a way to stop him from getting his pension benefits. "Jesus Christ Rolf, you are killing me!" I replied and finally, as the plant was nearing a complete stop, *ordered him to comply.*

Begrudgingly, he went over for the testing, but fifteen minutes later I received a phone call from human resources that under questioning, Rolf freaked out at the detail that was being asked and stormed out. I found him at his workstation and I told him that the testing is not a requirement and if he chose not to get tested, it would be okay. Of course, Rolf came back with "So management does not want me to take it?" as if he had been caught in a trap. "Oh my God, Rolf, you have been here twenty years." With that, I was summoned to a phone and was told that I also needed to get tested, so over I walked.

I was still shaking my head at Rolf's suspicions as I entered the office. There were still a few of my workers there, drinking coffee and chatting it up with the office girls, even though they had completed the testing. I was just about to get into it with them when a small woman wearing a funny hat called my name and, with snapping fingers, motioned me into the conference room. I gave the boys the stink eye as I was hustled into the glass room and asked to take a seat. There was a bit of a pause as she looked me over and then started to ask a few simple questions. After each answer, she hummed and hawed a bit as if she was already formulating an opinion.

I figured she was one of those clinical psychologists and saw right away why Rolf would become suspicious. She went on to ask me about my age, general health, marital status, any current relationships, my relationship with my children, and personal goals. I was stunned but answered each question as best I could. I could not believe the information required for a simple pulmonary test and I was starting to think Rolf had been right all the time.

The questioning went on for some time and then she asked if I had ever watched the reality show "Survivor?" I thought for sure this was leading into a series of situational questions and answered that I had never watched the show but knew the object of the game and what it brings out in human nature. She nodded as if to commend me and I smirked back as if I understood where she was going with this line of questioning. Then there was a long silence as if she was trying to construct a situation.

Then, she asked "Well, why don't you come over on Wednesday night to my place and we can watch it together, I just live across the road from you?" I started to reply but was not sure what the question was and after a few seconds of stammering I stopped myself and just sat there looking stupid. Finally it hit me that I was being asked out for a date with the psychologist and, totally floored, I agreed and as quick as that I was rushed back out to the main office to wait for my testing.

I was still not quite sure what had happened when my name was called again and I was pulled back into another office and a woman introduced herself and said she was going to ask me a few questions and then I was going to be tested. I told her that I just answered a whole bunch of questions from the other psychologist. She looked confused and told me that there was no other psychologist, she was not even a psychologist. So I asked whom had I been talking with and she, looking confused and a bit worried, said she had no idea. Then she quickly asked me my age and weight and sent me in for testing. So, in leaving the office there were two things on my mind: the first was the psychologist and the date, and the second was that Rolf refused to answer two questions—his age and weight.

When I got back to the plant I went to see Rolf and yelled at him in a mocking tone. "Your age and weight, two things—what are they going to do with your age and weight?" He replied, "They already had my name, so that was three things," as if they were going to triangulate some reason for deportation. Storming off, I went into my office and phoned human resources about this woman and was told that I had been talking with Katie. "Who," I asked "is Katie?"

Lori got up and shut her door and then told me that Katie worked in the forestry department in the basement but had been off for some time getting treatment for cancer. She had just returned and was told that there was a single guy her age at the plant and she should meet him. So, "Katie being Katie" heard I was coming in for some testing and took me aside for an interview. "So she is not a psychologist?" I asked, and Lori laughed and said, "What gave you that idea?"

After a few episodes of Survivor, some short walks and long talks, we began to get intimate. Here were two people who loved to be with each other but were entirely out of tune with each other sexually. Katie, who was recently divorced and had a grown daughter, knew that because of the cancer she may not have long to live and with that she just needed certain things in a certain way. She wanted intercourse, straight up, and she wanted it every night at least twice. She did not want to waste time with any foreplay and even kissing was frowned upon. Position-wise, it was missionary, but in saying that, she wanted it hard and fast and if it could be performed in a distant, almost cold manner, even better. She was not going to perform any oral "treats" as she called them and I was certainly not expected to perform any on her.

Now, while Katie was drumming out the conditions of our copulation agreement it sounded reasonable to me, but I quickly found that her expectations far outweighed my ability to deliver. I had been separated from my wife for about three years and in that time I did not have any sexual partners, so I was thinking Katie would take this into consideration and allow a ramp-up in activity. This was not to be. As soon as we agreed we would have sex it was game on. Well, this is a man's worst fear, but no matter how I tried I could not get an erection with Katie just lying there picking her teeth with a piece of cardboard. I tried to talk openly to her about it and she said she was patient and could wait, but she was not and could not. So the anxiety grew quickly and suddenly I could not sleep with worry that perhaps that was the end for me.

I started to read up on performance anxiety and thought if Katie understood it and could play a role in the cure she would. Well, she looked at me with a sour expression and came back with, "Oh, so you want to cuddle?" And then she gave me a bear hug and started to chuckle. It was hell to me, but to her she quite enjoyed my torment. We tried many times, but she would come up with things like, "I have heard that some men your age have this problem." She kept going on with "men your age" this and "men your age" that. I told her to please stop saying "men your age" as it was not helping.

One evening she seemed to want to chat about it, so, excited that perhaps this would lead to some softening and romance on her side, I sat up. She suddenly seemed to exhibit some understanding and showed a slight bit of empathy. She went on in exceedingly long sentences, now trying to avoid the phrase "men your age" about the problem and it seemed to me that she was willing to inject some minor degrees of foreplay into the mix. I was instantly buoyed.

So there on the couch we started to fool around a bit and this led us to the bedroom. Undressing, we started to kiss and a few gentle moves and things were instantly beginning to improve, if not actually physically as of yet, certainly I was starting to become aroused. I mean she was showing about as much affection as one would while changing a flat tire, but at least it was something. She was probably reading her mail behind my back or thinking about buying new floor mats for her car, but I was starved for affection and just her simple naked embrace induced a prowess within me.

Of course, Katie, in hearing my purring, would keep looking down to see if all that droning was resulting in anything solid. Even though she looked like she was impatiently standing in line for a bank teller, I could feel the juices starting to flow and in trying to persuade her even more, I whispered something naughty in her ear. She flinched away as if she was being pursued by a horsefly and then cocked her head to face me directly, like a staring contest. As the gyro was now beginning to gain some momentum, I had the urge to not just have intercourse, but to ravish her and all that tension and fear began to fall away. With a fire beginning to burn in the furnace, I was caught up in the swell of passion and growled out her name in a deep, earthy tone. "What?" she replied in a loud, granite response.

Trying to ignore her, which was difficult as she continued to stare me in the eye like a mongoose, I felt my bottom lip quiver and she started to chuckle and with a large smile said, "Wow, you are really into this." Though the moment was not entirely lost, I had misplaced it for a few seconds; she wanted to see that lip thing again and was patting me down like a cop, trying to find the

keremeye'us

erogenous zone responsible for it.

Desperately trying to get her off of that subject, I softly asked her, "Katie, what has come over you?" I was not actually looking for an answer at that time, but Katie began to chatter on about what she had discovered regarding "your problem" and "the female can play a role in helping a man your age with his problem" and so on. I tried to kiss her a couple of times just to shut her up but she dodged and snapped her head back as if I was trying to force feed her. All the time going on about "it being not entirely a physical disease like AIDS" and "it is also psychological, like a child molester or a serial killer." The fact that I was able to deflect her rambling and continue to build some momentum is a testament to how damaged and pathetic I was.

But I managed to zone her words out and from deep in my loins I felt the current now begin to swell. Though I was not listening at all to Katie's chatter, somewhere in the distant rhetoric she mentioned the "girls at work." Well past those sentences and onto "surgical erection implants", the words "girls at work" echoed about in my head, displacing the animal lust neurons firing like Desert Storm. Unable to dislodge "girls from work," I tried to repeat it verbally in a playful recount of what she was saying as if I was actually listening to her. "Oh Katie," I crooned, "What do the girls at work have to do with it?" I tried to nibble on her neck and let out a playful giggle. "Well, some of the girls in the office think you should get some pills," she replied. I went cold. "But accounting thinks it is psychological and that you need some professional help," she continued, adding, "purchasing thinks maybe you need a spanking or perhaps a vibrator up your butt, but they were joking, I think."

Frozen, I stood there looking at Katie ramble on, naming each department and voicing each girl's opinion on the matter of my sexual dysfunction. Unable even to breathe, I collapsed on her every word as the entire universe imploded around me. I sat there gaping in disbelief that the entire plant was privy to my worst nightmare and had been getting almost daily updates via the grapevine regarding my inability to perform. I was a frontline supervisor in a union plant, a position where any weakness is exploited and magnified as leverage and any means justifies a successful end and now it was common knowledge that I "could not get it up!" Stunned, shocked, dumbfounded, astonished, ashamed, speechless, and embarrassed, I needed to be alone. Katie asked me where I was going and stated, "You were doing so well?"

I wanted to kill myself. I sat in the darkness of my rented room for three straight days, only emerging to go the kitchen for food once while my landlady was at work. Katie was immune to such sensitivity and was off visiting her daughter and most likely doing an interview on a cable network about me. I never felt depression like that and seriously thought about packing up my shit and driving away. The thought of going to work and facing everyone was more than fear, it was physically debilitating and I just spent hours curled up in the foetal position on my bed.

As the start of my shift neared I became ill and threw up any food that I had managed to get down. I had not slept nor performed any personal hygiene and the light hurt my eyes; I was a shadow. Struggling to get dressed, I forced myself to drive to work and essentially hid in the far end of the warehouse for four days, avoiding any contact with anyone.

By the end of my block, I decided that I was going to seek some medical help and made an appointment at the local clinic. Swimming in shame, I sat in the waiting room for my name to be called, thinking everyone there knew the purpose of my visit. Once into the examining room the doctor quickly asked me what the problem was. I don't know where I started, but I think I began to give him my entire history, starting with my boyhood, in an attempt to avoid the real reason for my visit.

As soon as I started talking the doctor flipped out his pad and scratching a few lines, ripped off the small sheet and gave it to me. Standing up, the small Irish doctor slapped his hand against the bend of his elbow such that his forearm stood straight up. "It will be like a rock," he smiled and walked out. I looked at the pad and though it was hard to read, the words "erectile dysfunction" stood out. Even though I was appreciative to get some pills, I was

keremeye'us

thinking that some anti-suicide counselling or at least a pamphlet might accompany it. It was not and I was jostled off my stool and out of the examining room by a large native woman with six small children.

Unable to fathom that a simple pill could solve the problem, I stood in line at the pharmacy and had the prescription filled. Once home I stood naked in front of the mirror in my room and stared at my penis. It was no longer my best friend and poked out like a stub of a broken tree branch, lacking emotion or fervour. It seemed to belong somewhere else or to someone else and I stared at it for thirty minutes, waiting for the medication to work. Rather than exploding into a shaft, it reacted to the chill of the basement floor and sank almost inside of me, much like a turtle's head. I started to weep and let out a long and prolonged tragic howl, which resulted in the landlady banging on the floor above me.

Katie arrived back the next day and she had lots to tell me about her visit, so for a couple of hours it was a pleasant diversion from the elephant sitting next to me. We eventually got on to the subject of how we had separated the week before. I was not actually meaning to entertain her, but when I told her about the all the torment I was going through, she laughed until finally, I started to laugh also. It was a comedy, but a tragic one and for the rest of the night we giggled until the early morning hours. At some point, I said that we have to induce some sort of playfulness into the relationship, other than her laughing at my pain all the time. So, after some conversation I said we should have pet names for each other. She was all over that and right away sat straight up and wanted to make a list.

I was honestly just after a pet name for her, so we tried to find one that fit. I am sure we went through a hundred when I said "How about Peaches or Pudding or Lamb Chop." She jumped right out of the bed and said she wanted to be called "Lamb Chop." I was taken back a bit, but we were in "baby step mode" here and I said, "Yes, I will call you Lamb Chop." Katie was ecstatic and whirled about and then said, "You can call me Lamb Chop and I will call you Pork Chop!"

Joseph Woodcock

I begged her and begged her, but from then on it was Pork Chop. I mean I never actually ever did call her Lamb Chop—I hated the whole fried meat comparison—but she addressed me as Pork Chop everywhere we went. She introduced me to her daughter, her mother and father as Pork Chop and each time, she laughed uncontrollably with that rich, deep cackle. Half-laughing, half-crying, I wanted this to end. I both loved her and at the same time, I hated her guts, and she loved that I felt that way.

But, no matter how much we loved to be with each other, we still had not managed to seal the deal and now with this whole Pork Chop thing, I was terrified even to talk to her about any further additions. Katie often went to visit her family and for treatment and without me being able to satisfy her sexually, I felt she might be having a physical relationship with someone there. My suspicions were confirmed one day when she said to a friend of hers as we were all eating at the dinner table together that she had met a great guy and was having a sexual relationship with him. You would think I would be floored, but with Katie, it just comes out and I nodded and asked for her friend to "please pass the ham."

Something told me that if I did not mount Katie soon that our relationship might be in trouble. So I decided that I would go for the Hail Mary and put everything on the line the next evening. We were going to be alone and the situation was a positive one, so I prepared to take an overdose of erectile medication and collected up all of the lotions and creams, guides, picture books, and videos that people had given me and began to prepare. I wanted to be in character, so I tried to be cold like Clint Eastwood in High Plains Drifter and moseyed over to Katie's. Being as distant as I could, I motioned her up the stairs to the bedroom.

A few minutes later we were on the bed. I had timed that everything would come to a peak, medication wise, right at that time and, with my crotch swimming in lubes and extracts, I went right into action. Immediately, as I started to grind and rub, I could feel the blood pulsating to my little buddy. Katie was elated and began to urge me on. After just a few minutes of foreplay we actually achieved technical intercourse. Then tragically, Katie started yelling "Goooooo Pork Chop, go, go, go Pork Chop go!" and continued to yell everything pork related.

Immediately recognizing the danger, I tried desperately to cover her mouth with my hand, but she fought back laughing, "I am not into that choking thing, Pork Chop." Now I started to laugh and was begging her to "shut the fuck up," but she was heaving and contorting with hysteria. In full panic, I tried to kiss her but between her tears and runny nose, all I got was teeth. After about thirty seconds of her calling me Pork Chop my little buddy was heading back into his shell and suddenly, we were technically not having intercourse. There was about a ten second pause and then we both burst into laughter and between the tears I asked her, "How was it?" adding, "I bet you will never forget that!" We laughed so hard and for so long that we were almost sick.

A few days later we packed up her things into her car. She was relocating to another town. Soon she moved in with a guy and within a year they had married. I visited a couple of times and we kept in touch, each goodbye came with a hug and the words, "I miss you Pork Chop." Katie passed away soon after that and I presented the eulogy at her service a few days later.

Joseph Woodcock

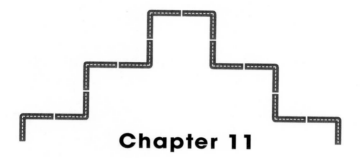

Chapter 11

I booked passage on a coastal supply vessel from Rimouski on the south shore of the St. Lawrence to Blanc-Salbon on the border between Quebec and Labrador. The N/M Nordik is a converted seagoing tug and for several days and nights I enjoyed the scenery of the isolated shoreline. There was a mix of passengers on board, some locals jumping from one outport to another, and others like myself who wanted a chance to feel a bit of the isolation of that area. As we set out from Rimouski the Captain explained to the passengers that this was a working supply vessel and therefore lacked any luxuries. Though the food and accommodation were exceptionally good, pulling into a remote village and loading and unloading freight in the middle of the night was the norm. But those who had booked passage were well-seasoned in this type of travel and at meal times we all sat together. It was marvellous to hear their adventures from around the world.

One such pair was an elderly married couple from the US. He was a fishing enthusiast and she was a painter of fast waters and together they ventured into remote camps and locations all over North America. Watching their vehicle, loaded with equipment, being lowered onto the deck of the ship with the crane, they gave an appreciative nod to the Captain and came below. They garnered instant admiration as most in their age were living out their last years walking the dog or waiting for the newspaper.

Two days into the voyage, as we sailed out of a fishing village in the Baie de Jacques Cartier, the fog cleared and we slipped by the outer islands, past tiny, desolate fishing cabins perched on the rocks. As we entered the gulf, large swells pitched and arched the vessel as the sea spray rose and fell upon the decks. Climbing the steep stairs, the passengers revelled in the excitement and huddled together on the upper decks, allowing the wind and salt to sting their eyes. Taunted by the sightings of dolphins and whales, the elderly couple climbed the stairs and, as the vessel fell below the shadow of the swells and then as it rose again, she lost her footing and fell backwards down the stairs.

In a tiny cabin on a working coastal supply ship, along the quiet northern coast of the Gulf of St. Lawrence, he the fisherman and she, a painter of fast waters, said their last goodbyes to each other. The crew had done their best to save her for several hours as the vessel raced for a harbour. Then, coming to rest upon the steady rise and fall of the swells, the engines fell to a slow idle. For a long period we drifted in silence and allowed the motion of the sea to carry her spirit away. Later, in the galley, we rose our glasses to her as someone read a prayer. Though solemn and quiet, we all wished for such an end, to be with someone you love, doing what you love.

We arrived in darkness and I collected up my equipment and got a room for the night at a local hotel. Not knowing what the next day would bring, I tried to get a sense of the area as I laid out my maps on the bed. Feeling the desolation, I now wished I had kept my tent as the heavy rains thundered on the parking lot under the yellow glow of the single streetlight. I had slept so much the past days that I spent much of the night listening to the wind sweep by the window and the distant cries

Joseph Woodcock

of shorebirds.

In the morning, I was having a cup of coffee and felt somewhat amazed that a rain of such magnitude was still thundering down. Heavy sheets of continuous torrent seemed to fall sideways against the windows of the restaurant and the murky vision of the bay and treeless hills faded in and out. Thinking it may blow over, I asked the waitress if the weather was going to change. Quite startled, she jumped back and looked out the window and replied, "Change to what?"

Her response, which was sincere, reminded me of a great Canadian film I saw when I was in middle school. The short animated piece was about stick people that lived on a sheet of paper in a two dimensional world, so they could see and move on two axes, the "X" and the "Y". One day there was quite a commotion because one of the stick people thought that he was being watched. No one could understand his paranoia as there was no one to the front, back, above, or below him, but he felt perhaps there was something else out there. The fear that there was something different than what they always knew terrified the stick people.

The waitress' reaction to my question was as if I had presented to her the presence of a new dimension or realm. It was clear that the weather I was looking at was absolute and to speak of something else was heresy.

Stepping out from under a torn canopy, the rickshaw and I were instantly whipped away, like a tern into the tempest. Seconds later I turned and searched for the hotel, but it, along with the horizon and any sense of direction, were gone.

I had thought that I might spend some time in Labrador, but it was clear that I was ill-equipped for venturing out into the wilderness under continuous fog and rain. So, after spending the day enjoying the local attractions, I took the ferry over to the northwest shore of Newfoundland. The weather was the same, but the western coastline was dotted with small outports and settlements.

Newfoundland and Labrador speak a distinct dialect of

English and if there is just one person speaking you can generally catch what they are saying, but if more than one person is talking it is almost impossible to understand. In the outport communities, isolated from outside influences, I had trouble understanding even one person talking. Several times I was invited into homes for dinner or to stay the night and even though they are talking at me continuously, I actually had no idea what they were saying. But aside from that, they are the friendliest people in the world. Being flagged in to some tiny clump of isolated cottages by a large un-kept man wearing gumboots, pajama pants, and a crop top exposing most of his belly would, in almost any world, set off some alarms. But in the outports of Newfoundland and Labrador it means you are welcome to come in and stay for as long as you want.

The only thing to match the people is the sheer beauty of the land. The entire west coast of Newfoundland is a treasure, and for three weeks I walked from St. Barbe to Port aux Basques. Most of the nights I was able to find a bed to sleep in, but the others were spent under that crazy little tarp I kept instead of my tent. The weather didn't change; as the waitress in Labrador said, "Change to what?" But long hours on the beach under my tarp, or trying to dry clothes over a large fire, felt therapeutic. For two days the wind blew so hard that I was not able to travel and I drank tea as I watched driftwood blow down the beach.

One day, not expecting any services at all, I found a small restaurant at the side of the road. It was mid-afternoon and I was standing in the doorway just about to read the lunch specials. A woman began speaking, but I was having trouble understanding her, so I just nodded. Setting a place and dropping a cup of strong tea in front of me, she threw a few things around in the kitchen before coming out with Seal Flipper and Burnt Toast. I laughed, as it reminded me of my mom.

Once a month or so Mom would make Scottish Chinese Food, which essentially was a few oriental noodles with everything in the fridge mixed in. It was her way of cleaning out and using up and though it was lovely with bread and butter and a cup of tea, if you watched what she was throwing in there, it would be hard to eat.

My mom was all about the basics and that included basic education. Though there were a few exceptions, my mother did not think much of new age teachers. In my first year of high school, which taught only grades eleven and twelve, I had a math teacher who was the son of a prominent family in town that owned the local hardware store. He was an excellent person and a dedicated and patient teacher. When the year began, he told the classes that he was going to give a test every two weeks and if you did not pass one, well we would work together and try and address the problems. But, he said, if you fail a second one, then he must place a phone call to your parents just to inform them, as they didn't want anyone to fall behind. He was always there to offer assistance before and after school and his students were successful and appreciative because of his dedication.

Those were difficult years for me at home and, dedicated or not, he had a real challenge ahead of him. After the first two weeks of school, we had a test and I failed. He took me aside and worked with me and did all he could. Two weeks after that, after the second failed test, he took me aside and said he was going to phone my parents that night. So I hung around the phone until it rang and then closing the bathroom door, I pretended I was my father, who was not even living there. I told him, in a deep voice, "Joe said you were going to phone. It is my fault as I have given him too many chores." Then, still in the low voice, "Thank you so much for your concern." That bought me two more weeks. But after failing the third test, he looked confused and said he was going to call again.

That night my mother was drunk and in a terrible mood; she was looking for a fight—any fight. I had forgotten about the phone call and was hiding in the living room when it rang. My sister, who was always hovering about the phone, picked it up and told my mom it was for Dad or her. My mom listened to my teacher go on and on about Joey and how he is failing math and then she blasted him with, "You fucking teachers—underworked and overpaid. You should all be placed in a gas chamber and given a shower, you fucking waste of skin." On it went for several minutes, my mother

keremeye'us

screaming at my poor math teacher who just wanted to do good. Then, as her tirade was exhausted, she told him to "never fucking phone again," and finally, "Joe is a big boy. He can make his own decisions. He has hair everywhere." And then she slammed down the phone and took a long drag of her cigarette. "He has hair everywhere." How eloquent. The next day my teacher, looking dishevelled, called me to the side of the room and said, "Joe, you are on your own."

It is both comical and sad, but that was the way it was. When I moved from primary school to middle school, my mother made me wear my older sister's baby-blue slacks with no fly and an elastic waist to my first day. Holy fuck, talk about fresh meat—it was a blood bath. I mean, I looked like a male ballerina. "Hey, drop that Hindu and look at this guy" was the first thing I heard as I walked through the gates alone.

Then just two weeks later, I arrived late for homeroom and ran in apologizing to the teacher. Trying not to draw any further attention to myself I quickly sat down. Everyone, including the teacher, was stunned to see I was wearing bright red lipstick. I complained the night before that my lips were chapped and my mother, not about to buy anything, used an old stick of greasy red lipstick to aid in the healing. I started to complain, but she cuffed me up the side of the head and went into a tirade about wasting money. Of course, we slept in and waking in a panic I rolled out the door and ran to school.

There was no sense in complaining—even to escape was demeaning. Years before, I'd had enough and packed up a few things and ran away. I lived on the edge of the Cowichan River for four nights, hiding from everyone as I thought there must be a massive search taking place. I dove for cover from all planes and lived off of crayfish and frog legs until finally, exhausted, I decided to return home and face the wrath. As I neared home I was sure I would be mobbed by search dogs and media, but after staggering the last mile, I ran into my mom and dad on their way to the Legion for the meat draw. Pulling up in the Dodge Power Wagon, my dad said, "Hey, dough head, when you get home, mow the lawn." I

Joseph Woodcock

was nine!

When I reached the Stephenville area I enjoyed a couple of short days and then, well rested, I pulled my rickshaw seventy-two kilometres in one long day, reaching the small settlement of Doyles at midnight. I had travelled the last hours in the pitch black, through the Codroy Valley in an incredible rainstorm and throwing that stupid tarp over a picnic table, I crawled into my wet sleeping bag. In the morning though, I awoke to clear skies and ate a hearty breakfast at a local restaurant before leaving the mouth of the valley and turning east toward Port aux Basques.

With the Long Range Mountains to my left and the Atlantic on my right, I walked through Wreckhouse in disbelief. The winds are so strong there that, in years past, trains were blown from their tracks. Near Billy's Pond I asked the only resident for some water. Beaming, he filled my water sack with clear, cold spring water from "dem 'ills" and gave me a hug.

I arrived in Port aux Basques in the late afternoon and after a good lunch, checked the ferry schedule. Hampered by weather at North Sydney, the ferry was running six hours behind, so I spent my last hours talking with the locals and exchanging adventures with other travellers. I arrived on Cape Breton late and walked off the ferry into a warm, calm night. It was too late find any accommodations so I stretched out on a bench along the foreshore park and watched the sun rise over the bay.

I was enjoying the warmth of the early afternoon sun along the water when I heard some yelling and screaming. The glass exploded from an apartment window and as smoke funnelled out a man climbed onto the ledge. His upper body was black and he had tied his belt to something inside and was dangling over the busy street as people scurried below him trying to help in some way. I took the opportunity to record the entire event on my cell phone camera. It may seem somewhat cold that I would not jump right in to assist a man hanging from his belt from a burning building, but I knew my limitations regarding fire.

keremeye'us

When my daughter was about thirteen, candles and candle parties were all the rage and she and my wife had candles burning all day long. I had tried to tell them of the danger, but really, Muffy had more influence than me and my words fell on deaf ears. One evening I was not able to sleep and told Kitten I was going to try the couch. So, with Muffy at my feet, I drifted away to dreamland on the couch in the living room.

My daughter, always behind a closed door, had fallen asleep with a liquid candle burning on the nightstand beside her. Sometime in the night, the thin bowl broke and the liquid flowed out with the burning wick onto the table and caught her bed on fire. Smoldering away, the toxic smoke filled the top half of the room. Her duvet was made of polyester and began to melt and burn her foot. Awakened by the pain, she sat up and breathed in the smoke. I am not sure what took place then, but I heard my daughter scream, "I'm on fire, I'm on fire!"

From the end of the driveway, I stood there in my underwear holding Muffy and watched through the window as my wife battled the flames to save our children. When I heard her screams, I had grabbed the pooch and ran down the stairs, out the door to the safety of the yard. Like I told my kids the next morning, under their stares of disappointment, "Someone had to secure the muster area and ensure clear access for the fire engines."

So with that on my record, I felt it better for me just to stand back and record the situation and let that old lady in the walker catch that man who was going to fall at any second. Later on, after the fire crew was mopping up, I showed the video to the fire chief. He said, "Oh, did you get the part when we arrived?" Not saying a word I showed him the video right from the start of the incident, including the long minutes of people desperately pleading for anyone's assistance. "Please, please, can anyone help us...anyone, anyone at all?" the words cried out from the camera phone. Quite overjoyed with the quality, I mean you could actually see his grip starting to slip, I asked the chief, who was stunned, "Do you think I could sell it to the local TV News?"

Joseph Woodcock

I spent the better part of a week near the Sydney Harbour area and took in the Coal Mining Museum at Glace Bay and the incredible Fort Louisburg. The weather was hot and days easy, reading in the mornings and napping away the afternoons. By week's end, I was walking slowly along the lazy shores of Bras d'Or, a beautiful inland sea, enjoying the pace and swimming in the warm waters. One afternoon, after taking a dip in the clear, salty waters, I watched a young blonde girl playing with a bucket in the sand. Her parents watched her closely from the shade of the woods nearby. Other children played farther down the beach and her solitude and physical appearance reminded me of my sister Cathy when she was young.

Cathy, who was just a couple years older than me, was tormented by us boys since I could remember. Her being over-sensitive only made our torture of her all the better and, sandwiched between me and three older brothers, she was constantly harassed and bullied. My mother would have to invoke a type of martial law every now and then decree a "be nice to Cathy day," which only made our persecution of her harsher once the day had passed.

There was no limit to our abuse of her. One day, with my parents out somewhere, my brothers Allan and George stood on her toes and each took hold of one of her arms. Standing spread-eagle she wailed as I, five years old, pulled up a chair to her and, standing on it, drove her in the face as hard as I could with my fist. We all agreed that she had sustained her injuries from walking into a door. It seemed to my parents as a plausible cause because she was always falling down or injuring herself in some way or another. She was a perfect victim as she knew what would happen if she ever told the truth. Generally diminutive and silent, Cathy was mostly a shadow.

One summer the circus and carnival came to Revelstoke, setting up along the dark banks of the Columbia River. It was 1965 and the people operating the rides and show were a mix of transients and immigrants of mixed origins. The entire town took in the attractions and rides, which lasted well into the night. Near eleven o'clock our family piled into the Rambler and my father

keremeye'us

turned and counted heads. As soon as he turned back to start the car, my brother Allan opened the car door and pushed Cathy out on to the ground.

We pulled away and drove through the desolate streets and up the CPR Hill to our house. We staggered in one by one we all fell into bed. About an hour later my parents woke to a knock at the door and opening it, found my Aunt Vickie holding Cathy. My Aunt Vickie and her family, just about to leave the carnival, had found Cathy wandering around the fairgrounds crying.

Across from our home in Revelstoke was an old sawdust pile from a sawmill operation many years before. The trees and brush had grown up through it and its consistency was almost that of soil. My brother Allan and his friend decided to dig a vertical tunnel to China but after some time became irritated at their slow progress. On queue, Cathy appeared and they decided to take out their frustration of her—they made her stand in the hole and filled it in around her so that her head just stuck out.

The sawdust pile was full of ants and grubs that had been dug up and Cathy started to cry. To muffle her, Allan placed an old red fire bucket over her head and he and his buddy ran away. Sometime later, as we had our lunch at the picnic tables, you could hear the faint wailing cries of our sister trapped under the bucket, slowly being devoured. I of course was privy to the prank, and along with the other boys, giggled with excitement.

The torment and torture continued right through her childhood and into her early teens. She was by then, a nervous wreck and at thirteen my older brothers forced her to watch the Texas Chainsaw Massacre at the drive-in. They then abandoned her alone at home, and came back at three in the morning to fire up a chainsaw outside her bedroom window. These kinds of things, along with the disintegration of any remaining sanity regarding normal family life, nudged her into marrying at age sixteen in an attempt to gain some peace and predictability.

At age seventeen, with my mother fleeing to England and my father working away, Cathy was placed in charge of me. Any distance and harmony that she had found was lost as she tried

Joseph Woodcock

to construct rules and boundaries to a fourteen-year-old who had never had to recognize any restrictions throughout his entire life. On many nights Cathy drove endlessly in search of me in her various attempts to reign me in. I was a veteran of disappearing, and though I was still active with the naturalist groups and worked at odd jobs, I was used to freedom and days and nights would slip by as Cathy worried about me. It was not fair to her, but fairness, along with other basic expectations were a distant myth.

Finally reaching Port Hawkesbury, I crossed over the jetty from Cape Breton Island and edged along the waterfront for another few days before pulling into Antigonish, Nova Scotia. In a downtown park I pulled into the shade of a large deciduous tree. I enjoyed an ice cream treat from a vendor propped up against its trunk and listened to the laughter of children playing nearby. There was a slight breeze, but the air was humid and small lines of sweat crept down my back. It was a good place to be I thought, chasing the melting ice cream down the stick with my tongue and I closed my eyes and welcomed the rest. Slipping away into a soft sleep I lay in the shade for an hour, the slight rustle of leaves and murmur of traffic woven within the peace of my dreams.

As the afternoon crept by I thought of my trek, the miles and months behind me then. My mother always said, "A little adversity never hurt anyone," but the journey never felt like a task, rather it had been an opportunity, a privilege. I remembered my breakfast a year earlier in Marquette, Michigan and the question posed to me. The restaurant owners had asked me if I could share with them the defining moment in my journey. The phrase "defining moment" stalled my response as I tried to gather the words to explain a feeling, rather than an event or single experience.

After a long pause, I answered the question. It had been in late February and the storms of the previous days had passed. As I walked out of the coastal mountains the valley began to open up. The river, no longer compressed between the slopes, began to wander and sway and the shadow of the hills gave way

keremeye'us

to digital blue. The Pacific swell, pushed upward against the westward side, had fallen as snow in gluttonous dunes. Trapped between the ocean and the fortress of the peaks, the storms raced inland through narrow chinks and had rushed down the eastern valleys.

Diminished of their heavy cargo, the winds painted the dry grasses white, polishing the desert as a crystal stone. Wincing at the glare, I walked easy in the relative warmth of the sun along the Similkameen. The first peoples called this place Keremeye'us and in thousands they lived there before, in thousands, they died. They held back the Europeans, burying the bones and armour of the Spanish before the silence of the invisible death took them away. Reduced from thousands to just a few, the valleys now carried only their echo.

Along the undulating rise and fall of the road, I had spent the afternoon enjoying the vistas. I rested upon a hilltop and looked out over the valley and rows of vineyards, dormant against the soft coil of the river below. They noticed me first from miles away. They noticed not only my rickshaw but also my easy pace, unfamiliar even in this land of soft days and quiet nights. As I boiled water for my tea, singles joined into a group as they walked up the hillside to greet me. They were pruning the vines months ahead of harvest and in the February cold the image of that harvest seemed as distant as the land they were from.

They were new Canadians and only one who spoke English well. The conversation went back and forth as he inter-preted and explained as best he could to others in the group. I was asked some questions, but my answers seemed to explain nothing. As the interpreter did his best, the group seemed agitated and pressed him to ask the same questions over and over. Almost embarrassed, he dwelled upon my past responses, listening to each word as if to find its meaning. I was answering his queries, but clearly there was a disconnect, and it was not just the language.

I was telling them that I was taking a walk, a journey of

unknown time and destination. I was saying that I was not on this journey seeking funds and was not sponsored by any organisation or group. I told them that I had worked in the north for the winter but had quit after saving enough funds for the season ahead. They had asked if I could go back to the job I had left and in reply I shrugged. These answers seemed to foster a slight distrust and, irritated, they pressed the interpreter for clarity.

Trying to formulate a motive for my walk, I realised that no matter what my response, the answer would not hold meaning. I was trying to explain that I was simply enjoying the most basic right, the right of freedom. As new Canadians, they understood the benefits of citizenship, which, they thought, came at a price and after years if not generations of labour. I was essentially telling these people that I am rich, but everything about me looked poor.

The word freedom has been altered to reflect only monetary wealth and discards the richness of family, health, and happiness as minor footnotes in the journal of one's entire life. I was trying to tell these new Canadians that not only is it possible to work hard every day and build financial wealth, but it is also just as acceptable to not do that. It is the freedom of choice; the daunting goal of always having to have more than those beside you is a trap, portrayed through media and commercialism in every part of our daily lives, and it serves only those who project it.

While trying to explain to this group of new immigrants the reason for my walk, only then did I realise the true value of having that right. When the interpreter was able to convey that I was celebrating my freedoms by the simplest of means it struck a chord both with the group and with myself. Being born in Canada it is easy to state that we are free, but this freedom is fragile and rare.

The journey for me would become just that: a celebration of my freedom. It was what I rose to each morning and saw each day in the mountains and wide prairies. It was the

keremeye'us

reason I seemed to smile during times of adversity and slept so soundly at night. Knowing the worth and value of those freedoms gave me confidence and I think my projection of those freedoms helped and inspired others. People often thanked me. "For what?" I would say. Some were not able to answer and just thanked me again and walked away. It was a feeling that defied definition to me for a long time until that afternoon at Keremeye'us.

Lying under the trees in Antigonish, I thought of the biker in Michigan who walked for miles to find me and then, wearing his heavy boots in the torturing heat, pulled the rickshaw for miles more. When I took his photo and offered it to him, he declined as he was seeking a feeling of freedom and no representations of any kind could quantify even a small piece of the actual.

Under the large shade tree, I decided that this was a lovely place and a good time to end my walk for that season. In a year from then, I would be trekking the Caminos of Portugal and Spain, but for now this would do and, waving the vendor over, I bought another ice cream and savoured the freedom.

Joseph Woodcock